Hurricane from the Heavens

THE BATTLE OF COLD HARBOR,
MAY 26 - JUNE 5, 1864

By Daniel T. Davis
and Phillip S. Greenwalt

EMERGING CIVIL WAR SERIES

Chris Mackowski, series editor
Kristopher D. White, historical content editor

For Bob,
Thank you for all your efforts
in preserving our history.

Hurricane from the Heavens

THE BATTLE OF COLD HARBOR, MAY 26 - JUNE 5, 1864

By Daniel T. Davis
and Phillip S. Greenwalt

EMERGING CIVIL WAR SERIES

SB
Savas Beatie
California

First edition, first printing

ISBN-13: 978-1-61121-187-0

Library of Congress Cataloging-in-Publication Data

Davis, Daniel T., 1982-
Hurricane from the heavens : the Battle of Cold Harbor, May 26-June 5, 1864 / by Daniel T. Davis and Phillip S. Greenwalt.
  pages cm. -- (Emerging Civil War series)
  Includes bibliographical references and index.
  ISBN 978-1-61121-187-0 (alk. paper)
  1. Cold Harbor, Battle of, Va., 1864. I. Greenwalt, Phillip S. II. Title.
  E476.52.D38 2014
  973.7'37--dc23
  2014005579

SB

Published by
Savas Beatie LLC
989 Governor Drive, Suite 102
El Dorado Hills, California 95762
Phone: 916-941-6896
Email: sales@savasbeatie.com
Web: www.savasbeatie.com

Savas Beatie titles are available at special discounts for bulk purchases in the United States by corporations, institutions, and other organizations. For more details, please contact Special Sales, P.O. Box 4527, El Dorado Hills, CA 95762, or you may e-mail us as at sales@savasbeatie.com, or visit our website at www.savasbeatie.com for additional information.

For Grandmom & Nana
"A grandmother is a little bit parent, a little bit teacher, and a little bit best friend."
—Unknown .

We jointly dedicate this book to
Chris Mackowski and Kristopher White

Table of Contents

List of Maps

Maps by Hal Jespersen

Federal cavalry attacked along this road on May 31 to open the way to Cold Harbor.

Acknowledgments

The book may only have two names on it as authors, but we had great support from friends, colleagues, and mentors throughout the whole process. First, Chris Mackowski and Kristopher White, who the book is jointly dedicated to—thank you for including us in the Emerging Civil War family and for your continued support, editorial eye, and camaraderie. We are indebted. Kris was also gracious enough to write a gripping foreword to the book. As for the rest of the ECW cohort: a greater bunch of friends and historians one cannot find.

Co-author Phill Greenwalt at the grave of an ancestor who was mortally wounded at the outset of the Overland Campaign, now buried in Arlington National Cemetery. (PG)

We thank Shawn Woodford and Christian Fearer for being part of this project. Their appendices greatly add to this history. Bert Dunkerly of Richmond National Battlefield helped immensely in this project while also working on a joint project of his own as part of the ECW Series. Ben Anderson, also a ranger at Richmond National Battlefield Park, helped us better understand the June 3 attacks of the V and IX Corps. Finally, Richmond National Battlefield historian Robert E.L. Krick assisted with questions on an elusive cemetery at Cold Harbor. Retired National Park Service historian Donald Pfanz continued to show why he is one of the nicest and most renowned historians living today. Hal Jespersen did a remarkable job again with the maps while handling questions and edits and deciphering those requests into great, clear, and concise maps.

Theodore Savas and Sarah Keeney at Savas Beatie have made the publishing effort seamless. We are honored to work with you.

Our good friend Kristin Simmler braved the August heat and accompanied us to Cold Harbor and Totopotomoy Creek.

Once again, we thank the people who shaped us and helped us become who we are today:

Dan: As always, to the love of my life, my beautiful wife Katy. Your patience and support are a great inspiration. To my parents, Tommy and Kathy Davis; my brother, Matthew; and my entire family for your continued support. Finally, to my grandmother, Cecilia Davis, for all of her enthusiasm, encouragement, and love. I know you are watching out over us still.

Phill: I am a very lucky man to have such a beautiful, understanding, and inspirational wife. Thank you, Adel, as you continue to inspire me and allow me to spend so much time in the distant 1860s. To the greatest immediate family, my parents, Stephen and Melanie; along with my sister, Adrienne; and brother, Patrick— thank you for your continued support and love. I would be remiss if I did not include a line thanking the great friends from WJU who have continued to support and encourage me: "Cardinals for life!" Lastly, to Nana, who I know would have read this book between listening to broadcasts of the Baltimore Orioles. Her whole life serves as an example on how to take whatever situation you are faced with, set a determined path, and love unconditionally.

PHOTO CREDITS:
Battles & Leaders (B&L); Dan Davis and Phill Greenwalt (DD/PG); Hanover County Parks & Recreation (HCP&R); Library of Congress (LOC); Chris Mackowski (CM); National Park Service (NPS).

Looking up toward the Confederate position from the south bank of Totopotomoy Creek (PG)

For the Emerging Civil War Series

Theodore Savas, publisher
Chris Mackowski, series editor
Kristopher D. White, historical content editor
Sarah Keeney, editorial consultant

Maps by Hal Jespersen
Design and layout by Chris Mackowski

Touring the Battlefields

To provide a comprehensive overview of the battle of Cold Harbor and the campaign that the engagement culminated, this book deviates from the National Park Service driving tour. Directions located at the conclusion of each chapter will direct you from site to site. Some of the sites will match up with the Park Service driving tour stops, while others will take you off park property and onto a mixture of state and private lands. Please follow all directions and posted signs and speed limits, as the driving tour will wind you through suburbs of Richmond and also around the busy Mechanicsville Turnpike.

The Cold Harbor visitor center is operated by the National Park Service as part of Richmond National Battlefield. There are exhibits about the battle, a bookstore, and restroom facilities, and historians are available to answer questions. (PG)

The narrative of the book begins on the banks of the North Anna River, although that site is not part of the tour. If you would like to visit the North Anna River, directions to the site are included with Appendix C.

The tour outlined in this book coincides with the narrative beginning with chapter three and the action at Haw's Shop leading up to Toptopotomoy Creek. From the visitor center, which is tour stop one, follow the directions to Salem Church, which is tour stop two. Directions to subsequent tour stops will be found at the end of each chapter.

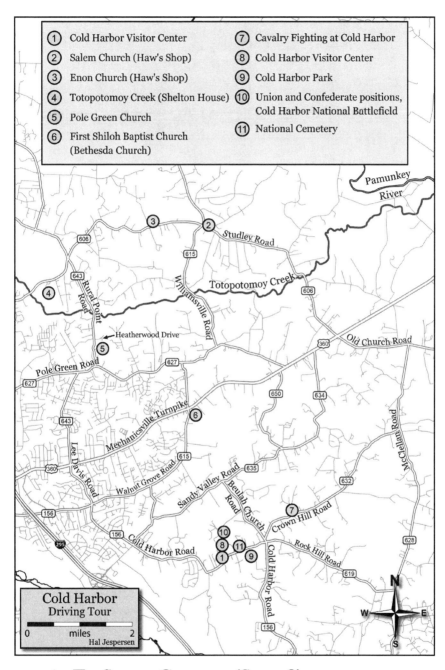

⟶ TO SALEM CHURCH (STOP 2)

Make a left out of the visitor center parking onto Old Cold Harbor Road (Rt. 156) and follow for approximately one-half mile. In 0.9 miles, bear left onto Crown Hill Road (Rt. 632). Remain on Crown Hill Road for 3.7 miles. At the intersection with McClellan Road (Rt. 628), turn left. In 1.6 miles, turn left onto Old Church Road (Rt. 606) and follow across the Mechanicsville Turnpike (Rt. 360). In approximately five miles, the destination will be on your right.

Foreword

BY KRISTOPHER D. WHITE

Major General George Gordon Meade glared unbelievingly at his young and rising star, Maj. Gen. Gouverneur K. Warren. "What have you done?" quipped Meade, "Why have you failed me? What are you doing here?"

Warren, Meade's II Corps commander, had taken it upon himself to call off what would have been the climatic assault of the Mine Run campaign (November 27-December 2, 1863), a campaign designed to bring Confederate Gen. Robert E. Lee and his outnumbered and outgunned Army of Northern Virginia to grief. "The enemy knows of our plans," the outspoken and self-righteous Warren claimed. "They had concentrated 40 guns on our position, and not a man could reach them alive."

Warren had, in fact, made a prudent game-time decision. Lee's army was happily ensconced behind a wall of earthen fortifications that offered clear fields of fire and numerous obstacles for the Federal attackers to overcome. The assault, in Warren's eyes, was a forlorn hope that would have inflicted grievous and unnecessary casualties on Meade's finest corps. Dejected, Meade ordered the Army of the Potomac to withdraw back across the Rapidan River and into winter quarters. As Meade did so, he told Warren, "You have ruined me."

Meade's failure to follow up his victory at

From the cemetery of Salem Church—the site of Haw's Shop (CM)

Gettysburg and the nearly four months it took him to go on the offensive against Lee weighed heavily on the mind of President Abraham Lincoln. His principal army, the Army of the Potomac, had failed time and again to take the Confederate capital of Richmond or decisively destroy the South's principal army. Mine Run was the last straw for the President. Something had to be done to right the ship.

The trenches of Vicksburg— where Grant earned his place as Lincoln's go-to general (LOC)

Lincoln's gaze often turned to the war's Western Theater, where an overabundance of Union victories was helping to cripple the South's ability to wage war. By early 1864, the president's gaze was squarely fixed on 41-year-old Maj. Gen. Ulysses S. Grant. Grant had quietly become the winningest general in Lincoln's stable. In 1862, Grant had taken the forts of Henry and Donelson and then went on to rip victory from the jaws of defeat at Shiloh. In 1863, he maneuvered and fought a masterful series of battles to bring the Confederate bastion of Vicksburg to its knees. Later in the year, he was called on by Lincoln to break the Confederate siege of Chattanooga, Tennessee.

By March of 1864, Lincoln was calling on Grant again. This time, though, Grant would command all of the Union forces in the field and hold the rank of lieutenant general—the first officer to hold the full rank since George Washington.

One of his first orders of business was to meet with the head of the Army of the Potomac, George G. Meade. On a rainy March 10, Grant arrived at Brandy Station, Virginia, the winter headquarters of Meade's army. Meade expected to be relieved of command, and to this end, Meade told Grant not to hesitate with the decision. "No one man should stand in the way of selecting the right men for all positions," Meade conceded. The gruff Keystone State general could only wait with baited breath for Grant's reaction.

The new three-star general played his cards close to his vest at all times, which prompted his close friend William T. Sherman to say, "To me he [Grant] is a mystery, and I believe that he is a mystery to himself." However, Grant was rather impressed by Meade, claiming later that this heartfelt admission "gave me a more favorable opinion of Meade than did his great victory at Gettysburg the July before." Grant chose to keep Meade in place.

The commanding general also chose to make his headquarters with the Army of the Potomac rather than in the Western Theater or in Washington. Grant would command all of the Federal forces from the front while acting as a security buffer between Lincoln's principal army and Washington's meddling politicians.

With the 1864 Presidential election looming on the horizon, Grant gave the green light to the campaign that would forever change the face of the American Civil War—and warfare—all together. The Overland Campaign of 1864 was to pit Meade's and Lee's armies against one another yet again. "Lee's Army will be your objective point," Grant told Meade. "Wherever Lee goes, there you will go also." The plan was to destroy Lee's army, which, in turn, would allow the Army of the Potomac to take Richmond.

Grant did not stop there. He also ordered two more armies to campaign in Virginia, one applying pressure in the Shenandoah Valley, the other pressuring Richmond. More armies would strike the Deep South, one slicing from Tennessee into Georgia, while another drove through Louisiana. Pressure would be applied across the board, which hopefully would bring the war to a swift close.

In the first week of May, the Army of the Potomac crossed the Rapidan River. The plan for Meade's army was to make a two-day march through the Wilderness of Spotsylvania and

Orange counties. Once through the Wilderness, Grant and Meade hoped to do battle with Lee's men in open fields, where the 123,000-man Army of the Potomac would crush Lee's 66,000 Rebels.

As Grant came to find out, Lee was a different kind of foe than any he had faced before. Unlike Grant's western opponents, Lee and his army knew how to fight—and how to win. Lee's battle-hardened veterans were ready for what was coming. "General Grant will go down like the rest of the Yankee Gens, that have bin brought against this army," penned one Georgia soldier. Walter Taylor of Lee's staff remarked that, "He [Grant] will find, I trust, that General Lee is a very different man to deal with."

Lee did not wait for the enemy to come to him, nor did he conform to the Federals' plan. Rather, Lee took his undermanned army into the Wilderness and met Grant and Meade head on. If he could throw Grant back across the Rapidan, he could take to the offensive as he did a year earlier. It was not to be. For two days the opponents slugged it out in the ugly tangled Wilderness, where the Federal numbers hampered their own movements. When the two inconclusive days of fighting ended, Grant was still south of the Rapidan and Lee was still staring him in the face. The first battle of "Grant vs. Lee" had ended in a tactical Confederate victory.

Undaunted, Grant ordered Meade out of the Wilderness, but unlike other Union commanders before him, Grant ordered an advance rather than a withdrawal. Grant would "fight it out on this line, if it takes all summer."

The armies clashed again at Spotsylvania Court House. Through oppressive heat and then heavy rains, the two armies battered away at one another. Lee grudgingly tucked his army behind earthworks. Grant ordered assault after assault against them. Innovative infantry tactics were created and employed to some success on May 10 and May 12. Rather than using a wide battle front, the Federal forces utilized a narrow-front approach, giving their assault depth rather than width. This in turn allowed Union forces to bore through the

Confederate lines. Though successful to a point, Lee was still able to counter every Federal move.

Again, after two weeks of inconclusive fighting, Grant ordered Meade's army south, ever closer to the Confederate capital. Lee won a race to the North Anna River, where he again entrenched, though this time he set a trap for Grant, which Grant nearly stumbled into. Realizing quickly that Lee had the upper hand, Grant again moved Meade's army south, ever closer to Richmond.

By June 2, the two armies lay some 11 miles northeast of Richmond. The Union Army held the crossroads of Old Cold Harbor, while the Confederates held the crossroads of New Cold Harbor. For days, Federal assaults failed to dislodge Lee's army, which held the inside track to Richmond. Grant unwisely believed that he had Lee's army at the breaking point and that one massive assault along the Confederate lines would kick the door open to the capital.

Grant was sorely wrong. Lee's men were in good spirits and in a strong defensive position, heavily entrenched along their entire front. Miles of fortifications lined the countryside—the most formidable works the Army of Northern Virginia had built to date. Open-field fighting was a thing of the past. In one bloody campaign, Grant and Lee ushered out open-field fighting—that standard way of doing battle since the time of Napoleon—and ushered in the trench warfare that would become the hallmark of the First World War.

Now in a strange twist of fate, Grant stood on the same precipice that Warren and Meade stood on seven months earlier. The Army of the Potomac was massed for an assault against a fortified line they had little hope of breaching, many taking time to sew their names to their uniforms. In the days before dog tags, it was one of the only ways they could be identified. Confederates waited in their trenches gazing across the no-man's-land. Like Meade at Mine Run, the next decision that was to be made would shape how history would view Ulysses S. Grant forever.

Kristopher D. White is co-founder of Emerging Civil War and serves as the historical content editor for the Emerging Civil War Series. White holds a master's degree in military history from Norwich University and is a former National Park Service historian.

"I never heard any one who was engaged there express a wish to see Cold Harbor again . . . .
It remains in memory the Golgotha of American history."

— *Lt. Thomas W. Hyde*
Union VI Corps

Prologue

A damp darkness provided a blanket to the many men who did not have one. Some of the New Yorkers tried to sleep while others sat on the rain-soaked ground, munching on a cold breakfast. The quiet rummaging for a plug of tobacco was broken only by noisy officers passing along the lines. A grey mist hung like a pall, making visibility extremely poor. Somewhere to their front, less than a quarter of a mile away, stood the Confederate breastworks. It would not be long before the regiment—the 113th New York—would have to move out into that pale abyss where every man's fortitude would be tested in the attempt to break the enemy line. The prospect left the men, one of them said, "sad of heart."

In July 1862, nearly two years earlier, President Abraham Lincoln had issued a call to the Northern states to raise 300,000 more men to sustain the war against the Southern rebellion. One month later, the 113th New York Infantry was mustered into Federal service. Since many of its recruits resided in Albany County, the unit was known as the "Albany County Regiment."

Heading the new regiment was Capt. Lewis Morris. Morris had served in the 1st U.S. Artillery and had distinguished himself in operations along the North Carolina coast. Morris came from good stock; his namesake and great grandfather was a signer of the Declaration of Independence.

A monument to the 8th New York Heavy Artillery stands at Cold Harbor National Cemetery. (DD/PG)

On August 21, the regiment arrived in Washington with the hopes of being assigned to the Army of the Potomac. Instead, they drew duty garrisoning the Washington defenses. In December, the unit was re-designated the 7th New York Heavy Artillery. The one-time infantrymen were now artillerists whose primary duties consisted of servicing the many heavy guns emplaced in the forts surrounding the capital. It was not until the middle of May 1864 that the regiment would be called upon to take the field.

Lieutenant General Ulysses S. Grant and the Army of the Potomac had engaged Gen. Robert E. Lee and the Army of Northern Virginia in the Wilderness and at Spotsylvania Court House. Grant desired to put every man possible in the field against Lee and had called upon the heavy artillery regiments in Washington. The gunners exchanged rammers and friction primers for muskets and cartridge boxes and then set out to join Grant. Arriving at Spotsylvania on May 18, the Seventh saw its first action the following day when they helped repulse a Confederate offensive at Harris farm. Their first exposure to combat quickly acclimated the regiment to the rigors of campaigning. "[I]t was their first fighting and it will do them good," one officer observed.

Unable to break Lee's lines at Spotsylvania, Grant sidled to the east. The two armies next clashed at the North Anna River. Assigned to Col. John R. Brooke's II Corps brigade, the Seventh was engaged in an attack on the Confederate lines there on May 24. Again, Grant was stopped, and again he moved east, this time toward the Pamunkey River. On the far side, and only some two weeks removed from the Washington defenses, Morris and his men were again skirmishing with Rebels—this time along Totopotomoy Creek.

Late on the first day of June, the "heavies," as they were known through the army, abandoned their lines. All through the night they marched, until the following morning when they reached a quiet Virginia crossroads known as Cold Harbor.

When the 7th New York Heavy Artillery attacked on June 3, 1864, they achieved something no other unit in the Federal army would achieve. (LOC)

The road junction was less than 10 miles from the Confederate capital of Richmond.

"[O]f all the wastes I have seen," a Federal staff officer wrote, Cold Harbor "was the most dreary!" One of the houses at the intersection was "wretched," and to the west was "an open plain . . . on the sides and in the distance were pine woods . . . it was Sahara intensified."

Morris directed his regiment into line on the left flank of the army. Orders had been given for a general assault to take place against the Confederate lines the next morning, June 3. A signal gun would announce the attack. The regiment had faced strong entrenchments at the North Anna, but what awaited them at Cold Harbor paled in comparison. A Yankee remembered that the enemy position was nearly "perfect."

Anxiously, the men waited through the night and into the wee hours of the morning. Minutes seemed like hours. At the beginning of the month, they had been in the comfort of Washington, not a one having heard a shot fired in anger. As they waited, each man knew that within hours there was a good chance that the man next to him would be no more. They were about to storm into the bloody crucible.

They did not know it yet, but later that morning, the regiment would accomplish something no other unit in the Army of Potomac could accomplish.

Grant and Lee
CHAPTER ONE
MAY 25, 1864

Morning broke with the smell of rain. The gray dawn shone through the tent, but as Robert E. Lee sat up, sharp pains knifed through his abdomen. Diarrhea had stricken the general at a crucial time, leaving him incapable of directing his vaunted Confederate Army of Northern Virginia. He had skillfully forced his longtime nemesis, the Union Army of the Potomac, into a position below the North Anna River that left it isolated and vulnerable—yet illness now crippled him.

Lee had been able to capitalize on such moments in the past. For nearly two years, he enjoyed almost constant success against the Potomac army and its string of commanders. In the spring of 1862, Lee was appointed to command Confederate forces defending Richmond. Re-christening them the "Army of Northern Virginia," he launched a series of attacks against the Union army, then under the command of Maj. Gen. George McClellan. The Seven Days battles secured the Confederate capital from the Federals. Later that summer, Lee defeated elements of the Army of the Potomac, along with Maj. Gen. John Pope's Army of Virginia, at the battle of Second Manassas. A Northern invasion in the fall ended in the bloodiest day in American history at Antietam Creek. Lee closed out the year with a victory at Fredericksburg over Maj. Gen. Ambrose Burnside. He opened the new campaign

Grant and Lee first clashed in the dark, close tangle of the Wilderness—and from there, the tangle continued across central Virginia in a nonstop campaign of fight and maneuver. The trail of casualties left in its wake was hitherto unprecedented in the war. (DD)

Known as "The Old Gray Fox" for his craftiness on the battlefield, Robert E. Lee found himself tested as never before during the spring campaign of 1864. (LOC)

season in May of 1863 with his greatest victory, over Maj. Gen. Joseph Hooker, at Chancellorsville. Despite suffering a defeat at Gettysburg the following July, Lee's army remained dangerous.

During the Seven Days, at Second Manassas, and at Chancellorsville, Lee had been able to launch grand assaults that contributed to his victories. At the North Anna, fate intervened, and the assault never came. "We must strike them a blow," Lee said from delirium. "We must strike them a blow!" enveloped Lee, but the blow never came. The great opportunity passed.

The loss of dependable officers, such as Lt. Gen. Thomas "Stonewall" Jackson the previous year and Lt. Gen. James Longstreet earlier that spring, had limited Lee's offensive capabilities. Debilitating illnesses suffered by Lt. Gens. Richard Ewell and A. P. Hill further hampered the Confederate high command. The victories of the past had depended on the acumen of the leadership of Lee's army. When the chief went down with an illness himself, the army did not have the leadership to capitalize on the advantage set for them at the North Anna.

*   *   *

Across the river, Lee's counterpart, Ulysses S. Grant, emerged from his tent and pulled on a frock coat. A medium-sized man with a full beard, Grant wore boards with three gold stars on his shoulders, signifying for the first time since the American Revolution that an American officer held the full rank of lieutenant general. Making his way to a nearby fire, he sat down to review papers. An officer handed him a cup of coffee. He reached into his vest pocket to produce a cigar, which was promptly lit.

One of the papers, a general order, drew particular attention. Putting down the cigar, Grant focused on its details. The document engrossed, and when his attention turned back to the cigar, its fire had burned out. Although he relit the cigar, the fire that burned inside Grant was far from extinguished.

Those flames had been raging since February of 1862 when Grant, then a brigadier general, kicked open the South's western door. His capture of Forts Henry and Donelson opened middle Tennessee to the Federals. Despite struggles through the remainder of the year, the following summer, Grant captured the city of Vicksburg and shut down the use of the Mississippi for the Confederates. By the end of 1863, Grant had relieved besieged Union troops at Chattanooga.

In March 1864, Grant was promoted to lieutenant general—a rank last held by George Washington—and given command of all the Union armies. Grant's plan for the spring campaign was for a concerted, coordinated advance against the Confederates across the entire country, from Louisiana to Virginia.

"I determined . . . first to use the greatest number of troops practicable against the armed force of the enemy," Grant later revealed, "to hammer continuously against the armed force of the enemy and his resources, until by mere attrition, if in no other way, there should be nothing left to him."

Grant decided that he would direct the operations from Virginia while traveling with the Army of the Potomac, still under the command of Maj. Gen. George G. Meade. He intended to be a bystander and allow Meade to direct operations against Lee.

Grant had met Lee only once before: following the U.S. Army landing at Veracruz during the War with Mexico. Each man learned the lessons of maneuver and assault from such officers as Zachary Taylor and Winfield Scott, applying those lessons to their own campaigns in Virginia, Tennessee, and Mississippi.

Initially, Grant told Meade he did not envision a campaign of maneuver. "General Grant," Meade predicted in reply, "you are opposed by a general of consummate ability, and you will find that you will have to maneuver for position."

Under Grant's orders, Meades army crossed the Rapidan River on May 4 and marched into a dense forest west of Fredericksburg known as the Wilderness. Apprised of the movement, the wily Lee marched out of his winter encampments and the

Soldiers in the Army of the Potomac withheld judgment on Lt. Gen. Ulysses S. Grant when he was appointed general in chief. "We are prepared to throw up our hats for him when he shows himself the great soldier here in Virginia against Lee and the best troops of the rebels," one Maine officer explained. (LOC)

"My duty is plain," said Army of the Potomac commander Maj. Gen. George Meade when he found out Grant would accompany Meade's army in the field, "to continue quietly to discharge my duties, heartily co-operating with him and under him." (LOC)

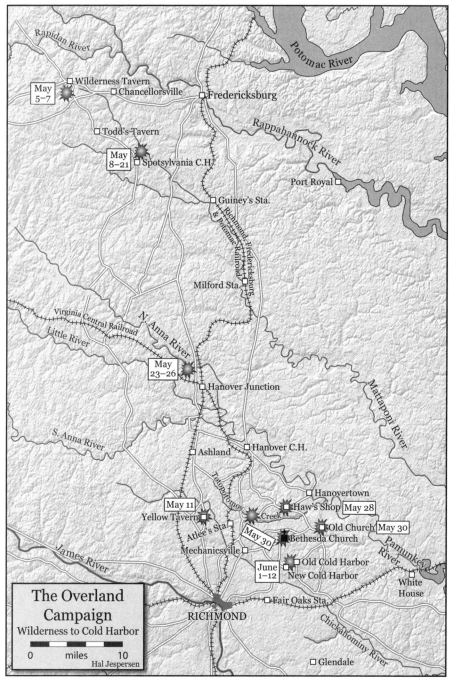

The Overland Campaign—Starting on May 5 with the fighting at the Wilderness, the Confederate Army of Northern Virginia and the Union Army of the Potomac began a running series of battles and maneuvers over 70-plus miles of eastern Virginia. Ulysses S. Grant had vowed "to fight it out along this line if it takes all summer," and Lee held him to it. The campaign witnessed extensive casualty lists on both sides as Grant edged closer to Richmond.

battle opened the next day. As the two sides positioned to meet each other, perceived dawdling and a lack of aggressiveness caused Grant to take a stronger hand in the tactical direction of Meade's army.

On May 5, the Overland Campaign opened when the armies first clashed in Saunders Field, one of the few open areas in the Wilderness. (DD/PG)

The pivotal fighting occurred on May 6. Early that morning, Maj. Gen. Winfield Scott Hancock's II Corps crashed into the Confederate right. Victory was seemingly in sight until Lt. Gen. James Longstreet's First Corps arrived. The ensuing Confederate counterattack stabilized the situation. Later that day, Longstreet launched a flank attack which shattered the Union line. In an amazing turn of events, Longstreet suffered the same fate that befell Stonewall Jackson the previous year at Chancellorsville. In the attack's aftermath he fell victim to friendly fire. Later that night, the Confederates launched another attack on the Union right, throwing the lines back in confusion and ending the fighting.

Lee had stopped the Yankees cold in the Wilderness. On the morning of May 7, Grant issued orders to "make all preparations during the day . . . for a night march to Spotsylvania Court House." This was a watershed for the Army of the Potomac. For the first time after being fought to a standstill, they would not withdraw. "There will be

By the morning of May 8, the two armies had maneuvered to the outskirts of Spotsylvania Court House, where Confederates blocked Federal advances across Spindle Field. (DD/PG)

no turning back," Grant had vowed at the start of the campaign—a promise he stuck to.

Grant hoped that by moving south to Spotsylvania he could break into open country and get between Lee and Richmond. Unfortunately for the Federals, the Confederates won the race to the critical crossroads. There, they dug in to await the next Union onslaught. Attacks came in fits and starts until May 12, when Hancock assaulted a salient in the Confederate line known as the "Mule Shoe." Initially successful, the attack soon lost steam and allowed the Confederates to counter. The fighting funneled toward a bend in the earthworks near the western end of the salient. Forever thereafter known as the "Bloody Angle," both sides engaged in hand-to-hand combat through a pouring rain until darkness set in.

The "Bloody Angle" symbolized the horrors of Spotsylvania, where the two armies engaged for another nine days. In the end, Grant decided to turn Lee's right. The goal this time was the North Anna River. Grant again hoped to get the Confederates in the open and threaten their supply lines.

Lee again foiled Grant's intentions. Like the march to Spotsylvania, Lee's army arrived at the North Anna ahead of the Yankees. On the south bank of the river, Lee ensconced himself behind tremendous earthworks in a formation that resembled an inverted "V." Grant wrote that an assault "would cause a slaughter of our men that even success would not justify." Thwarted again, on May 25, Grant examined his options.

Foremost in Grant's mind was being able to supply the army. A move to the west, around Lee's left would extend his supply lines and leave them vulnerable. Another march around Lee's right, to the southeast, would allow Grant to utilize the Virginia rivers to transport supplies. Additionally, it would place Grant closer to the Union Army of the James, which was actively campaigning against the city of Petersburg. The maneuver would present Grant the option of using the two forces to operate in concert against Lee.

Between Spotsylvania Court House and the North Anna River, the Federal army had to cross the Mattaponi River— one of several eastward- flowing rivers and creeks with high banks that acted as formidable natural barriers. (B&L)

On the morning of May 26, as he sat next to the campfire sipping coffee and smoking a cigar, Grant issued orders to begin the march that night. This time, the objectives were the crossings along the Pamunkey River, well east of Lee's North Anna fortifications.

Ever since the antagonists made contact on May 5 in the Wilderness, the war had turned savage in Virginia. The two armies had been in daily contact. The top military commanders—Grant and Lee— had traded punch for punch. Each engagement was highlighted by fierce fighting. The armies were bleeding dry.

Grant's plan to swing east seemed sound. However, Grant would limit the one trump card he had played time and again: maneuver. From the Wilderness to the North Anna, where the armies were currently stalemated, Grant had executed a march around the Confederate right flank to gain a more favorable edge. It had been the great equalizer. By shifting to the ground between the Pamunkey and Chickahominy Rivers, Grant would be severely

The Confederate earthworks at the North Anna battlefield are among some of the best-preserved earthworks of the Overland Campaign. Where once the Confederate position looked out across an open attack plain, today it looks out toward a tall grassy mound (seen in the distance through the trees) that marks the boundary of a gravel quarry. The gravel company donated much of the land that comprises the modern park, which is maintained by Hanover County. (CM)

condensing the area of operations. Grant believed that he would not be able to fight Lee in the open and restricting his movement could potentially limit future maneuvers should Lee be able to counter again.

Whether "Marse Robert" still had the capacity to effectively engage the Yankees was a matter of question. The inability of Lee to attack the Federals below the North Anna convinced Grant that the Confederate army was on the brink of collapse. "I feel that our success against Lee's army is already assured," Grant crowed to Washington. "Lee's army is really whipped." Unbeknown to Grant was Lee's illness, which was the only reason the butternuts did not sweep out of their earthworks and trap the Yankees against the riverbank.

Still, the pounding he had administered over the previous weeks was nothing like what Lee's army had felt up to this time in the war. In the past, Lee was used to having his way with the Union commanders sent against him. But Sam Grant was not George McClellan, John Pope, or Ambrose Burnside. The constant pressure applied by Grant

allowed him to retain the initiative, an element coveted by Lee.

James Longstreet accurately described Grant's tenacity prior to the beginning of the campaign: "That man will fight us every day and every hour until the end of the war." Longstreet's words could not have been more prophetic. In three weeks of fighting, Grant had inflicted over 27,000 casualties. It seemed that one final, concerted strike might be enough to break the Confederates.

As the armies inched farther and farther into east-central Virginia, Grant remained true to his overall plan to destroy the Army of Northern Virginia. Now, with the Confederate capital a stone's throw away, would Lee's army continue to be Grant's target? Would Lee be able to counter Grant's left hook yet again? Would Grant be forced to change his strategy?

These answers lay many days, and thousands of lives, in the future.

Once the Union army crossed the North Anna River, Grant realized they had stumbled into a trap. The men quickly entrenched to avoid calamity, then waited for the situation to unfold. (LOC)

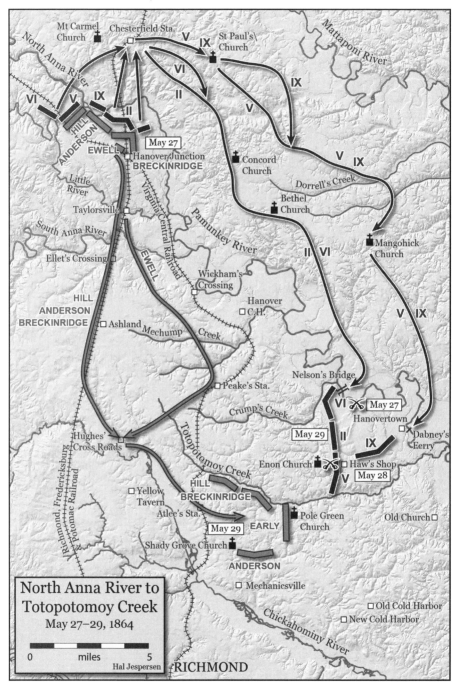

North Anna River to
Totopotomoy Creek
May 27–29, 1864

0   miles   5

Hal Jespersen

NORTH ANNA RIVER TO TOTOPOTOMOY CREEK—As he had done at the Wilderness and at Spotsylvania, Grant directed Union forces around Lee's right flank at the North Anna. The two antagonists shuffled south of the Pamunkey River, sparring along the way. The narrowing theater of operations gave Lee limited room to maneuver, but he nonetheless found a strong defensive position along Totopotomoy Creek.

At The North Anna River

Well-marked signage can direct you off of Route 1 toward the 80-acre North Anna Battlefield County Park located in Doswell, Virginia. From there, a trail with interpretive markers allows you to access some of the original battle lines and entrenchments. As you walk the trails of the state battlefield park, imagine peering down and seeing through the foliage, with an eagle-eye view, the vulnerable Union dispositions.

Consider the secret those hills and bluffs held as Grant looked at them—as did thousands of Union soldiers—and wondered why the offensive-minded Lee didn't launch an attack when Grant had unintentionally given him a great opportunity? He had no way to know that Lee's immediate subordinates were failing him even as Lee's own health failed him.

"We must strike a blow," Lee groaned from his sickbed. "We must never let them pass us again. We must strike them a blow." However, his subordinates did not take up the slack. Here at North Anna, Lee missed the late Stonewall Jackson as he admonished Gen. A. P. Hill, "Why did you not do as Jackson would have done [and] thrown your whole force upon these people and driven them back?"

Lee knew opportunities like North Anna were rare in warfare. He had learned that in Mexico with Winfield Scott. Now Lee would have to figure out Grant's next move—surrendering the initiative again—and hope for another opportunity like he had at North Anna. Would the next engagement give him a chance at redemption?

The North Anna battlefield has a trail with ten tour stops that feature excellent interpretive markers and an orientation kiosk next to the parking lot. The battlefield's only monument sits there, too: a bolder with a bronze plaque dedicated to "all the valiant men who lost their lives on the battlefields of the North Anna." The monument was erected by the descendents of Cpl. Michael Shortell of the 7th Wisconsin, killed at Jericho Mills on May 23, 1864. (CM)

March to the Pamunkey

CHAPTER TWO

MAY 26-27, 1864

A bedraggled set of Yankees shook themselves to life as they gathered for breakfast. Infantrymen munched on hardtack around campfires as they attempted to ward off the rain. The men of Brig. Gen. David Russell's VI Corps division would play a critical role in the army's movement to the Pamunkey River. "Colonel, let your men know that we are to have a hard march tonight, so that they may get as much rest as possible," Brig. Gen. Emory Upton told one of his regimental commanders, Elisha Kellogg. "We shall probably be within fifteen miles of Richmond by tomorrow morning."

To deceive Lee from his true intentions, Grant decided to send Brig. Gen. James Wilson's cavalry division west to demonstrate against the Confederate left. While Wilson kept the Rebels in check, Russell's division would withdraw from their lines below the North Anna River to Chesterfield Station and await nightfall. With the remainder of the cavalry corps under Maj. Gen. Philip Sheridan, Russell's men would march southeast to the Pamunkey, with the remainder of the army following in their wake. The cavalrymen would forge a crossing and establish a bridgehead on the south bank to allow the infantry to cross.

As Grant prepared to execute the maneuver, reports flooded into Lee's headquarters throughout the day from the First and Second corps, under

The Pamunkey River at Nelson's Crossing—one of two spots the Union army crossed to the south bank. (CM)

On May 27, the right flank of the Union army recrossed the North Anna River near Jericho Mills, where they had scored a success against A. P. Hill on May 23. (NPS)

Maj. Gen. Richard Anderson and Lt. Gen. Richard Ewell, respectively, of movement behind Hancock's lines. To determine what the Union forces were up to, Lee directed Anderson to forward skirmishers and make contact with the enemy. Anderson chose the division of Brig. Gen. Joseph Kershaw to undertake the task.

Kershaw directed his skirmishers to ascertain what, if any, Union troops occupied the entrenchments facing them. The movement brought them into contact with elements of Brig. Gen. Robert B. Potter's IX Corps Division, temporarily under Winfield Scott Hancock's charge, and the Northern soldiers responded promptly. A steady skirmish was kept up between the antagonists. When the news and gunfire trickled back to the Confederate high command, Lee interpreted this as support for his theory that the dogged Federal defense was to mask the movement of men from the Union left flank to the right.

Reports from the Confederate left flank seemed to provide evidence that Lee was correct in his assumption. A. P. Hill's Third Corps could see, from their vantage point high on the bluffs around the North Anna, straight down the Union line. What these observers saw was the movement to the rear of enemy wagons and Yankees scurrying about their camps in preparation. Wilson's pesky Federal troopers were also making quite the fuss.

Arriving at their jumping off point for the march to the Pamunkey, a surgeon in Russell's division remembered that his comrades "bivouacked in a pine wood." At dark, the division stepped off, bound

Lee charged Brig. Gen. Joseph Kershaw with probing the Union right flank. Kershaw's men had undertaken a similar reconaissance in force on May 15 at Spotsylvania, where they roughly handled elements of the Union II Corps under David Birney. (NPS)

for the Pamunkey. As Russell began his march, Grant began the precarious task of withdrawing from the lines below the North Anna. Throughout the night, the Federals quietly withdrew so as to not give away their movements to the enemy. Surprisingly, the army was able to get back to the north bank of the river with little molestation from Lee's army.

The approach toward Nelson's Ford—one of the routes the Union army took across the Pamunkey River (CM)

Meanwhile, Russell's division and Sheridan's cavalry had gotten underway. A Connecticut soldier described the march "in darkness and in silence, hour after hour, with a rest of more than five minutes at a time" the men were "hurled along that sandy road. There was no danger that the head of the column would lose its way, for a large body of cavalry had preceded us a day or two before and dead horses lined the road throughout. The darkness began to fade before the inflowing tides of the morning light, but the jaded men kept on."

As Russell's men marched through the night, Sheridan's troopers began arriving at the Pamunkey crossings. "Little Phil," as he was known, left some of Brig. Gen. David Gregg's men upstream to secure Littlepage Bridge, while Brig. Gen. Alfred Torbert's

Brig. Gen. David Russell had led the 7th Massachusetts Infantry during the Penninsula Campaign. Two years later, he found himself in charge of a division, again leading the charge "on to Richmond." (LOC)

Crossing the Pamunkey (NPS)

Brig. Gen. George Custer led the cavalry effort to hold Confederate horsemen at bay while Federal infantry crossed the river. (LOC)

division marched on to Dabney Ferry, arriving there before dawn. Torbert's assignment was to secure a crossing on the south bank and await the infantry. To achieve this end, he chose one of his brigade commanders, Brig. Gen. George A. Custer. Custer commanded four regiments from Michigan. Despite some opposition from enemy cavalry, the Wolverines were able to forge their way across. They would spend the bulk of May 27 skirmishing with their Rebel counterparts. Late in the morning, Russell's exhausted ranks began crossing.

Back at the North Anna as the sun rose that morning, the rest of the vast Union host was on the move, winding its way from the North Anna to the Pamunkey. Prominent amongst its ranks were Grant and Meade. The pair rode along together accompanied by their staffs. "[T]he soldiers by this time were getting on intimate terms with their commander," wrote one of Grant's staffers, Col. Horace Porter, remembering an incident with a private. "Is it all right general?" the soldier asked Grant.

"Yes," the general replied, "I think so."

One of Meade's staff officers recalled of the march. "We kept on, through a very poor and sandy country, scantily watered," he said. By early afternoon, the commanders reached Mangohick Church. It had already been a long two days, and the group elected to stop and set up camp. With the North Anna behind them, Grant and Meade would begin directing the rest of the army across the Pamunkey on May 28.

*   *   *

As Grant slipped away, Lee received reports that Union cavalry with infantry support had crossed the Pamunkey and pushed back the meager Confederate pickets in the area. In addition, Confederate lookouts and skirmishers had confirmed that there were no enemy troops on the south side of the North Anna River. Though unsure of Grant's objective, Lee realized he

The Federal crossing at Hanovertown (LOC)

had to act quickly and decisively. By midmorning the Army of Northern Virginia had abandoned its trenches at the North Anna and was headed southeast toward the Virginia Central Railroad.

Lee's mission was to place his army astride this important railroad near a small hamlet called Atlee's Station. This would put him in a prime position to block any enemy movement from the Pamunkey. Ewell's Second Corps left first, followed by Maj. Gen. John C. Breckenridge's division—which had arrived in the east from the Shenandoah Valley after a victory over Federal forces at the battle of New Market in mid-May. Anderson's First Corps marched next. Last to leave was Hill's Third Corps.

By nightfall, the Confederate advance had reached Hughes' Crossroads after tramping 15 miles. The march had been exhausting, even to these veterans soldiers. One Rebel remembered the march as "very disagreeable . . . the mud being up to our knees." What the foot soldiers did not realize, though, was the movement placed Lee right where he wanted to be.

Work remained, though, and orders went out that night to resume the movement to Atlee's Station. This time, the objective was Totopotomoy Creek where high ground would offer Lee a prime defensive position. Before the movement could commence, a change in command occurred for the Confederate army. Ewell, racked with dysentery, relinquished command to Maj. Gen. Jubal Early. Lee, on May 29, urged Ewell "to retire from the field that he may have the benefit of rest and medical treatment" and he ordered his subordinate to "proceed to some place where you can enjoy that repose and proper care." With those simple directives, Ewell—the heir-apparent to the late Stonewall Jackson and his former subaltern— left the Army of Northern Virginia,

Pontoon train across the Pamunkey (LOC)

never to command the corps again.

As both armies jostled for position and blindly felt what was ahead of them, one thing was inevitable: new horrors would be forged below the Pamunkey.

Along the Pamunkey

Built around 1795, "Wyoming" overlooks the approach to Nelson's Crossing. Henrietta Nelson—known as "widow Nelson"—lived on the 1,200-acre farm with her two daughters and several servants. Her son, Thomas, was a private in the 4th Virginia Cavalry; he would die in action on June 24, 1864. (CM)

The country that the Army of the Potomac traversed to reach the Pamunkey has managed to avoid massive development. The area looks much like it did in 1864.

The movement toward the Pamunkey can best be described by using basketball terminology. Like a great point guard, Grant—using Wilson's cavalry to deceive the enemy—had faked to his right and caught the Confederates looking to their left. Then, he put Russell and Sheridan in motion, like a basketball player switching hands, driving past the Confederate right. Now, the Confederates, like a defender who has lost the initial step, would have to recover and get in position to take the proverbial charge from the point guard. The question now: could the Confederates recover in time?

The Confederates were leaving behind at the North Anna River some of the strongest, most impressive earthworks constructed thus far in the campaign. Such fortifications were relatively new to each side. They were initially implemented by the Confederates as a means to offset the numerical superiority of the Federals. Theodore Lyman, a Union staff officer, wrote:

> *It is a rule that, when the Rebels halt, the first day gives them a good rifle-pit; the second, a regular infantry parapet with artillery in position; and the third a parapet with an abbatis in front and entrenched batteries behind. Sometimes they put this three days work into the first twenty-four hours.*

Construction began by digging a ditch, the earth thrown up in front towards the enemy and reinforced by logs. To this, the soldiers added firing steps as well as a head log that rested about a foot above the works to further shield the defenders, thus giving them a protected portal to fire through. Every 10 yards, additional trenches were built at right angles to the main line. These "traverses" protected against flanking fire. Finally, whatever trees that remained in the area were felled, their ends and branches sharpened and placed 10 to 15 yards in front of the line to aggravate an attacking enemy.

Beginning at Spotsylvania, a pattern began to emerge: Wherever the armies marched, each side would dig in after reaching their destination. Since the beginning of the campaign—just a matter of weeks—the earthworks had taken on a life of their own. In elaborateness, these fieldworks resembled small fortified cities. One veteran casually remarked that "Virginia will be one great network of them."

As the shift began to the hinterlands between the Pamunkey and Chickahominy Rivers, this evolution in warfare, these earthworks, would strongly influence the operations of both armies.

The Battle of Haw's Shop

CHAPTER THREE

MAY 28, 1864

Major General Philip Sheridan, commanding the cavalry corps of the Army of the Potomac, rose early on the morning of May 28. Standing just 5'5", Sheridan had a bullet-shaped head, and according to President Abraham Lincoln, "such arms that if his ankles itched he can scratch them without stooping." Sheridan had performed ably as an infantry division commander out West, and when Grant was appointed general in chief, the new commander brought Sheridan east with him and appointed him to command Meade's cavalry.

Thus far in the campaign, Sheridan had turned in a lackluster performance. His horsemen had failed to detect Lee's movement following the Rapidan crossing, which allowed Lee to surprise Grant and Meade in the Wilderness. Next, Sheridan's failure to clear the road from the Wilderness to Spotsylvania Court House resulted in a spat with Meade. Rather than discipline Sheridan, Grant dispatched him south in an effort to engage the Confederate cavalry. While the expedition resulted in the death of J. E. B. Stuart, it deprived the Federals of their eyes and ears at Spotsylvania and during the march to the North Anna, resulting in a number of missed opportunities for them.

With the Pamunkey and a mighty army at his back, it fell to Sheridan to hold the bridgehead south of the river and, most importantly, send back

IN MEMORY OF 27 UNKNOWN CONFEDERATE SOLDIERS KILLED AT THE BATTLE OF HAW'S SHOP MAY 28, 1864 AND BURIED IN THIS CHURCHYARD

A monument to fallen Confederates stands alongside the parking lot at the Enon Church. (DD/PG)

The death of Maj. Gen. J.E.B. Stuart (left) on May 12 left a hole in the command structure of the Confederate cavalry that Robert E. Lee had a difficult time filling— not because of a dearth of suitable replacements but because of an overabundance. South Carolinian Wade Hampton (center) and Lee's nephew, Fitzhugh (right), had both proven themselves highly capable. Both would find themselves outmatched by their Federal counterparts as the armies shifted toward Cold Harbor. (LOC)

intelligence on the whereabouts of the Confederates. "It became necessary," Sheridan wrote, "to find out by actual demonstration what Lee was doing and I was required to reconnoiter in the direction of Mechanicsville." As Torbert's division guarded the river crossings, Sheridan sent David Gregg's division toward the small hamlet of Haw's Shop.

If there was a time that Robert E. Lee sorely needed the late cavalry chieftain James Ewell Brown Stuart—and there were plenty such times since Stuart's death on May 12, 1864—it was on May 28. Coming from the North Anna, Lee's Army of Northern Virginia had moved southeast to block Grant's possible avenues toward Richmond. Now, Lee was concerned about where the Union army specifically was. He needed his cavalry to find out. Whether they would be up to the task was another question.

Since the night before, Maj. Gen. Fitzhugh Lee, the commanding general's nephew, had insisted that the Union thrust would come via Haw's Shop from their current positions around Hanovertown. To find answers, the commanding general directed the cavalry to precede east through Haw's Shop while the infantry headed south to their designated spots behind Totopotomoy Creek.

Now the cavaliers, who had once followed the plume of the late Stuart, mounted up and headed east. With the death of Stuart, Lee had declined to immediately name a successor. The choices came down to his nephew and Maj. Gen. Wade Hampton. Lee's indecision came not because he worried about either man's competency but because both men had proven themselves capable of the job.

Fitz Lee, born on November 19, 1835, in Northern Virginia, was the son of Sydney Smith Lee, an older brother of army commander Robert E. Lee. Serving in the cavalry since 1861, he rose through the ranks, proving himself a capable brigade and division commander and serving in all the campaigns of the Army of Northern Virginia's cavalry.

Wade Hampton was a wealthy South Carolinian. When war broke out, he helped finance a mixed infantry-artillery-and-cavalry command called "Hampton's Legion." His men fought well at First Manassas, and Hampton's star began its ascent. He had proven himself at Brandy Station and at Gettysburg, and by 1864, he had been wounded multiple times.

The upcoming operation would test the leadership of Robert E. Lee's cavalry. Complicating matters further, Hampton's vanguard was commanded by Brig. Gen. William C. Wickham. Wickham's brigade belonged to Fitzhugh Lee's division, and Wickham reported to him directly. Fitz chose to accompany the brigade eastward, convoluting the command structure even further.

As one additional complication, some of the cavalry were seeing their first action with the Army of Northern Virginia. A number of Confederate cavalry reinforcements had recently arrived from garrison duty locations in the Deep South. One of these regiments, the 4th South Carolina, arrived in Virginia with approximately 1,000 men. Veterans in the army mistook them for a brigade. One soldier remarked that South Carolina might be "a little state" yet could raise "big regiments."

The South Carolinians would quickly get a taste of not just combat but life in a campaigning army. Life was completely different than their duty back in their native state. Rations were "one-third of a pound of bacon and some corn meal . . . there being no coffee, tea, or other stimulant," one described. Virginia did not seem so welcoming to these new arrivals.

Maj. Gen. Phil Sheridan, commander of the Federal cavalry, had largely underperformed during the Overland Campaign, but strong performances by his division commanders during the march from the Pamunkey kept the Army of the Potomac well protected. (LOC)

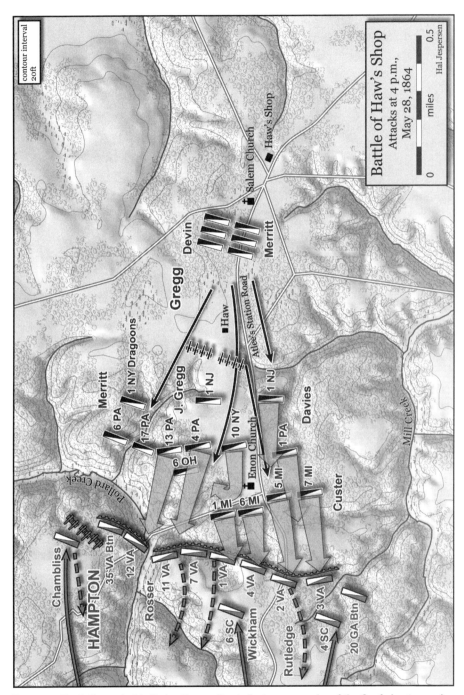

BATTLE OF HAW'S SHOP—In his first action as the de-facto commander of the Confederate cavalry, Wade Hampton fought an engagement at Haw's Shop against Union cavalry advancing from the crossings of the Pamunkey. Although pushed off the field, Hampton's men stymied the Union cavalry in the day-long action, buying valuable time for Lee's infantry to position themselves along Totopotomoy Creek.

From Enon Church, looking out across the Haw's Shop battlefield (DD/PG)

Making things worse, because of the precarious nature of Confederate resources, fewer than half of these new South Carolinian cavalrymen were mounted. Only those with mounts—some 300 or so men—were capable of joining in the expedition.

*   *   *

By sheer coincidence, the Confederate and Federal antagonists headed toward the same small Virginia hamlet. As it would become known, the battle of Haw's Shop was a meeting engagement—more or less meaning that both sides blindly collided.

After reaching Haw's Shop, Federal Brig. Gen. Henry Davies' men had turned west along Atlee Station Road. Riding on toward Enon Church, the Yankee horsemen ran into Wickham's Confederates. Davies' lead regiment was quickly driven back by the Rebels, prompting a countercharge. The battle seesawed around the quiet chapel. As each side fed regiments into the fight, the lines stabilized. Davies deployed his men on both sides of the road, just west of the church.

Some of Hampton's dismounted men had

Enon Church (DD/PG)

Although the battle resulted in a Confederate defeat, the tablet by Enon Church—erected in the 1920s by the Battlefield Markers Association—tells the story differently: "Confederate cavalry under Major General Fitzhugh Lee in a severe engagement withstood for five hours the Federal advance, thereby allowing the Army of Northern Virginia to take its position beyond the Totopotomoy." (DD/PG)

thrown up makeshift breastworks along their lines for defense, with the Union troopers advancing in small pockets against them. Colonel John Kester of the 1st New Jersey remembered it was "the severest cavalry fighting of the war." Gregg described it as "exceedingly stubborn."

"The enemy largely out-numbering the force which I had to engage, was yet unable to do more than hold his position, and from this he was driven at different points," Gregg attested. "For some hours the contest was thus maintained under a heavy and destructive fire, the lines of the contending forces being closely drawn up on each other."

For the latter part of the morning and into the afternoon, the two forces slugged away at each other, with neither side obtaining a decided advantage. Both sides funneled more cavalry units into the fray.

Around 4 p.m., the situation shifted in favor of the Yankees as Torbert's division began arriving in the rear of Gregg's lines. Released from his duty of watching the Pamunkey, Torbert headed for the scene of the fighting. Elements of Brig. Gen. Wesley Merritt's and Col. Thomas Devin's brigades reinforced Davies north of Atlee Station Road. Moving up to solidify the Union center was the all-Michigan brigade under George A. Custer.

Major James Kidd, commanding the 6th Michigan Cavalry, remembered the brigade's experience during the fight. "The men all dismounted and advancing up the road . . . formed in line of battle . . . then we advanced," he wrote. "In two minutes we were within two rods of the enemy . . . . They fought desperately but then had to give way."

A Confederate cavalryman understatedly remembered that we "had to cut our way out."

Custer's assault helped to break Hampton's line. An officer from the 2nd U.S. Cavalry wrote that "we pursued them some distance," but the day's fighting had exhausted the blue and gray both, and Sheridan did not press his advantage. The fighting climaxed around 6:00 p.m.

Hampton credited some of his veteran cavalry, the notable "Laurel Brigade," with withdrawing "without loss and in perfect order." Although this limited the casualty figures, each side lost slightly more than 350 men, killed, wounded, and missing. Of the 300 mounted troopers from the 4th South Carolina, 127 became casualties. The men from the Palmetto State now joined their fellow veteran regiments with their contribution to the bloodbath that was the Overland Campaign.

Following the battle, Little Phil decided to consolidate his lines around Haw's Shop. The first round of fighting below the Pamunkey had gone to the Federals, but the match had many more rounds to follow.

After the battle, George Custer set up his HQ in an area that now serves as the courtyard of Salem Church. (DD/PG)

At Salem Church

The settlement of Haw's Shop derived its name from a local family that manufactured farming equipment. At the outbreak of hostilities, the machinery was sent to Tredegar Iron Works (now the Richmond National Battlefield Visitor Center) to be used in the Confederate war effort. During the battle, Salem Church was turned into a hospital by the Federals.

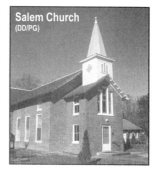

Salem Church (DD/PG)

⟶ TO ENON CHURCH (STOP 3)

Make a right out of the parking lot for Salem Church and proceed west 1.1 miles on Studley Road to Enon Church, which will be on the right.

At Enon United Methodist Church

At the climax of the fight at Haw's Shop, George Custer led the 6th Michigan Cavalry in a dismounted charge. Surging forward as the brigade band played "Yankee Doodle," Custer led his men through the area where you now stand toward the Confederate line, which was situated in the woods behind you and across the road. Mistakenly believing reports that his left flank was in danger, Hampton ordered a withdrawal. Combined with the assault of the 6th Michigan, Hampton's line collapsed.

The performance of the Union cavalry was crucial at Haw's Shop. By holding their position and driving away their adversaries, they were able to protect the infantry crossings along the Pamunkey and ensure that the bridgehead remained secure. Any penetration of Sheridan's cavalry screen would have spelled disaster. This would have opened a clear way to the Pamunkey and seriously threatened the Union forces as they were attempting to cross the river.

Confederate responses showed the state of the cavalry by the summer of 1864. Gone were the "knights of old" that the late Stuart emulated. Now, the Confederate cavalry valiantly tried to hold their own against superior numbers and weaponry. In addition, reinforcements to replace casualties were beginning to scrape the already scant resources of the Confederate War Department. The Palmetto State reinforcements needed in Virginia left Charleston less defended. Ironically, three years of war had taken resources away from Charleston when back in 1861 all eyes, manpower, and military accoutrements were headed toward that South Carolina port city.

Even with the disadvantages they faced, coupled with the defeat at Haw's Shop, the Confederates continued to espouse high morale. Can you imagine having low rations and tired mounts, facing men armed with seven-shot repeaters while you have a signal shot carbine, all while being outnumbered— and still entering voluntarily into an engagement? That is what the Confederate cavalry had to muster—and without an overall commander—in every engagement. Yet, said one of Hampton's horsemen, "The men of his corps had the same unwavering confidence [in Hampton] . . . that the 'Stonewall Brigade' entertained" for their former leader.

In the distance across the field, to the right, stands the former Haw residence, known as Oak Grove. During the battle, Federal troopers attacked from the direction of Salem Church, which is beyond Oak Grove. (DD/PG)

Shortly after the cavalry action near Enon Church, George Meade established his headquarters in this vicinity. Even later in the campaign, during their night march to Cold Harbor, Horatio Wright's VI Corps passed through.

→ **TO THE TOTOPOTOMOY CREEK BATTLEFIELD AT RURAL PLAINS (STOP 4)**

Oak Grove (CM)

Make a right out of the parking lot and proceed west on Studley Road. In approximately 2.5 miles, you will see the National Park Service signs on your left for the Totopotomoy Creek Battlefield at Rural Plains. The entrance to the parking lot is on the left.

The Battle of Totopotomoy Creek

CHAPTER FOUR

MAY 29—JUNE 1, 1864

While Sheridan boxed with Hampton and Fitzhugh Lee, the bulk of the Union army crossed the Pamunkey. "The country we were now in was a difficult one," Grant later wrote. "The streams were numerous . . . with impenetrable growths of trees and underbrush." An officer in Wright's VI Corps wrote, "Great is the shovel and spade . . . . I would as soon dig the Rebels out than fight them."

The general in chief was not of the same opinion of this subordinate officer. Rather than entrench and await the enemy, the ever-aggressive Grant decided to send out the Yankee infantry and find Lee.

Lee was waiting. He and the Army of Northern Virginia had ensconced on the south side of Totopotomoy Creek behind a line of earthworks they had thrown up along the crest of the steep bank that dominated its northern counterpart.

Major General Jubal Early's Second Corps guarded Shady Grove Road, just south of Totopotomoy Creek. His men had fortified a line just west of Pole Green Church. Behind Early, astride the road, was the First Corps. Continuing the line behind the water barrier on Early's left was John Breckenridge's division, which was encamped along Atlee Station Road. Well beyond Early's left was Hill's Third Corps, which covered the Virginia Central Railroad and the roads leading north.

Situated on the Totopotomoy Creek battlefield was the Shelton House—known as Rural Plains—which, in happier and more peaceful times, once saw the marriage of Patrick Henry to Sarah Shelton in 1754. The house was built in 1670 and served as the home for members of the Shelton family until 2006. (CM)

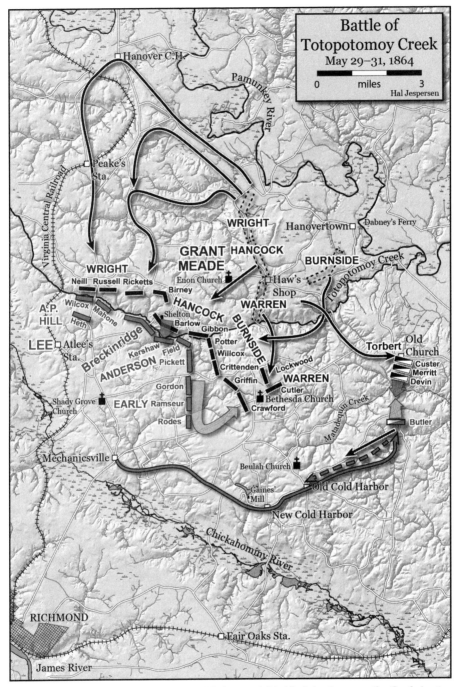

BATTLE OF TOTOPOTOMOY CREEK—Action swirled around this Virginia stream as the Confederates moved to interpose themselves between the Union army and Richmond. Spirited attacks by Jubal Early's Second Corps on May 30 and the Union assault across the creek on May 31 highlight the action. After inconclusive fighting, the strong Confederate defenses convinced Grant to shift his forces southward toward Cold Harbor.

Lee did not have long to wait. On the morning of May 29, the Federals began their reconnaissance. Advancing in the Union center were elements of Winfield S. Hancock's II Corps. Hancock had proven to be a reliable officer in the early stages of the war, but he had been hampered by wounds received at Gettysburg, and the Overland Campaign was beginning to take its toll on him. For the mission, Hancock chose Brig. Gen. Francis Barlow's division. In turn, Barlow sent his most aggressive brigade commander, Col. Nelson Miles, west along the Atlee Station Road.

II Corps commander Maj. Gen. Winfield Scott Hancock (top) sent in his most aggressive division commander, Brig. Gen. Francis Barlow (below), who in turn sent in his most aggressive brigade commander, Col. Nelson Miles (bottom). (LOC)

Reaching a local crossroads—Polly Hundley Corner—Miles ran into Confederate cavalry and began "pushing them steadily back." Miles advanced west along Atlee Station Road, past the stately home of the Shelton family, Rural Plains, and then descended a ridge. A Pennsylvanian remembered they encountered "a strong force of the enemy . . . behind [e]ntrenchments of a formidable character." Miles immediately sent word of the Rebel presence back to Hancock. While the rest of Barlow's division deployed along a ridge occupied by Rural Plains, Hancock ordered Maj. Gen. David Birney's division into line on Barlow's right. Intermittent picket firing continued throughout the course of the day.

Early the next morning, May 30, John Gibbon's division arrived to deploy on Barlow's left. "Our troops were moved close up to this line with constant skirmishing and artillery fire going on nearly all day," Gibbon wrote. He lamented the strength of the Confederate position. "A few hours were all that were necessary to render a position so strong by breastworks that the opposite party was unable to carry it . . . and when the enemy had occupied a position . . . ahead of us . . . it was useless to attempt to take it."

As Gibbon's soldiers wound their way into line, Col. John Tidball, the corps' chief of artillery, began placing his batteries along the ridge. Tidball recalled that his men "commenced throwing up works for artillery in front, and to the right and left

Hancock's other II Corps division commanders, Brig. Gen. John Gibbon (left) and Maj. Gen. David Bell Birney (right). (LOC)

of the Shelton house." Several Coehorn mortars were placed directly in front of the house.

As a diversion, Miles sent the 61st New York and a battalion of the 2nd New York Heavy Artillery forward to engage the Confederates. The Empire Staters "advanced to a crest overlooking the enemy's position and threw up breastworks under a severe fire from the enemy of musketry."

The ruse did little to divert the attention of the Confederates. Lieutenant John Roder, commanding Battery K, 4th U.S. Artillery, recalled, "The enemy's sharpshooters and their artillery annoyed me . . . . About 11 a.m. the shelling became quite severe. They opened with all their guns . . . . I directed Lieutenants Smith and Burnes to return fire, which they did with such accuracy as to compel the enemy's cannoneers to abandon their pieces. I fired 223 rounds of solid shot and shell. Had 4 men wounded."

A Confederate remembered some of those 223 rounds, recording in his diary that "one passed only two yards to the left of my company, splashing the mud all over us." Luckily the firing proved ineffectual, as the diarist indicated in his entry: "However, no one was injured."

Maj. Gen. John Breckenridge, former vice president of the United States, led Confederates to a victory on May 15 at the battle of New Market in the Shenandoah Valley. His men were then transferred eastward to provide much-needed reinforcements to Lee's army. (LOC)

Meanwhile, north of Atlee Station Road, Birney's Federals were mixing it up with their Confederate counterparts. One Union soldier recalled that they "advanced to within 800 yards of the enemy's line . . . under a heavy fire . . . . Quite a number of our men were killed or wounded."

Late in the day, Barlow ordered one of his

brigade commanders, Col. John R. Brooke, to assault the Confederate line. Brooke shook out the 148th Pennsylvania Infantry and the 7th New York Heavy Artillery for the assignment. An officer in the 148th Pennsylvania wrote that "his men joined a portion of the . . . line in a charge across the Totoptomoy." The heavies, as converted artillerymen, led the way, though, supported by the Keystoners. Brooke wrote the regiments "moved down the . . . slope . . . crossed the stream and assailed the enemy's strongly [e]ntrenched skirmish line, which, after a hard fight, was carried." Hancock proudly wrote that "Brooke's brigade advanced . . . over obstacles which would have stopped a less energetic commander and carried the enemy's advanced line of rifle pits." Darkness brought an end to the foray, though, and the regiments to return to their original position.

Artist Alfred Waud sketched the Shelton House. (LOC)

Lee was receiving reports from the front as scouts along the lines reported what they saw. Coupled with these were the observations of the "eyes of the army," the cavalry. This intelligence informed Lee that a large Union force was congregating across from the right of the Confederate line. Lee interpreted this as yet another flanking movement and sought to counteract this trend. He turned to Early's Second Corps. The First Corps under Anderson would also join in as needed.

The "Wily Old Fox" was emerging from his hole one more time, hoping to disrupt Grant's plans and retake the initiative. Stonewall Jackson's old command would be counted on again near a small hamlet church called Bethesda.

At Totopotomoy Creek

The Totopotomoy area has three distinct layers of history overlaid atop each other. It gets its name from Totopotomoi, chief of the Pamunkey indians. An ally of the British, Totopotomoi was killed in the Battle of Bloody Run, one the most notorious Native American battles in Virginia history. (CM)

Unfortunately, much of the Confederate position along Totopotomoy Creek has fallen victim to development. On the Federal side, the National Park Service maintains the area primarily occupied by Barlow's II Corps division.

The centerpiece of the property is Rural Plains, built in 1670. In October 1754, Virginia patriot Patrick Henry married Col. John Shelton's daughter, Sarah, in the front parlor. The family remained in the house throughout the time their property was occupied by Hancock's men. Much to the horror of Col. Edwin Shelton, who was serving in the Army of Northern Virginia, his family's house became the focal point of the artillery duel that occurred here on May 30. Shelton watched as Rebel shells struck

Two cannons positioned near the Shelton house represent John Tidball's line of artillery along the ridge. (CM)

The walking trail at Totopotomoy Creek goes past Rural Plains, some old outbuildings, several sets of Federal earthworks (left), and an old family cemetery (middle) before heading down to the creek itself. There, a bridge crosses the creek to the Confederate positions beyond (bottom). (CM/CM/PG)

Lt. Robert Robertson of the 93rd NY infantry fell seriously wounded at the battle. His journal is the basis for much of the interpretation along the walking trail. (NPS)

the house. During the bombardment, one of the Shelton slaves ran out into the yard and emptied a shovel of hot coals into a nearby caisson, igniting the ammunition inside and killing several Union soldiers.

The Shelton House remained in the family until

Totopotomoy Creek itself isn't as wide as many of the streams the Union army had to cross during its march south (left), but it meandered across a swampy bottomland that was difficult to cross (above) and its steep south bank gave Confederates another daunting position (below).
(CM)

2006, when it was turned over to the Nationl Park Service. Richmond National Battlefield manages 124 acres of the property's original 1,000—from the Shelton House down to the banks of the Totopotomoy. A two-mile walking trail covers the ground, which passes through several sets of Union earthworks, past the family cemetery, and down to the low, swampy bottomlands of the creek itself. A long walking bridge crosses the lowlands and connects with a trail that takes visitors up to the Confederate earthworks along the crest of the steep south bank.

As you climb the far rise, imagine being a Union soldier with the unenviable task of having to possibly

Remains of the strong
Confederate position
still wind along the crest
of the hills on the south bank
of the Totopotomoy. (CM)

attack that strong defensive network. Conversely, imagine looking down from those heights as a Confederate soldier, peering through the woods and the mists rising from the waterways, trying to discern what those blue-coated Northerners are doing. Small depressions and two-to-three-foot high rows of earthworks still snake through the battlefield.

A roadside monument along Route 606 near the approach to Rural Plains marks the location of the Confederate earthworks on the hills above. The marker is one of the famous "Freeman monuments," which noted Southern writer Douglas Southall Freeman wrote and helped raise funds for in the 1920s. Fifty-nine such markers dot the landscape around the city of Richmond and the surrounding counties of Chesterfield, Henrico, and Hanover. The markers consist of a cast-iron plate on a granite base. The original markers inspired similar tablets elsewhere. Another group, the Battlefield Markers Association (Western Division), took on the task of placing these same style monuments from the battlefields of Manassas to Appomattox. (PG)

→ TO POLEGREEN CHURCH (STOP 5)

Turn right out of the parking lot and proceed east for approximately one half mile. Turn right onto Rural Point Road (Rt. 643). In approximately 1.5 miles, you will start to see the white frame outline of the church's structural beams. Turn left onto Heatherwood Drive (Rt. 1750). After making the turn, the parking lot will be on the right.

At Polegreen Church

A marker explains the story of the destruction of the original church. (CM)

Polegreen Church was resurrected in 1995 as a memorial to religious freedom. (CM)

Polegreen Church is hailed as "the Birthplace of Religious Freedom in Virgina." The church derives its name from a local landowner, George Polegreen. The church was established in the early 1740s and, by the end of the decade, it was led by its most influential minister, Samuel Davies, who served as pastor there for the next ten years. The future Virginia Patriot Patrick Henry could be counted among Davies' congregation. The preacher's fiery oratory would inspire Henry to his own as he spoke out against the transgressions of Great Britain.

During the Civil War, Polegreen Church ended up between the opposing lines as the two armies slugged it out along Totopotomoy Creek. On May 31, Winfield Scott Hancock advanced his divisions. He recalled that his men "pushed up close to the enemy's line, but owing to the unfavorable nature of the ground could effect nothing more." During the advance, Rebel sharpshooters utilized a building next to the church to harass their enemies. Covered by soldiers from the 69th Pennsylvania Infantry, Pvt. Denton Lindley of the 106th Pennsylvania rushed forward and set the building on fire.

The next day, shells fired from the Third Richmond Howitzers struck and ignited the church itself. According to some sources, William B. White, pulled the lanyard that sent the fateful shell hurling into the church; ironically, White's father was baptized at Polegreen.

Following the war, the church was never rebuilt. Not until 1990 did the Presbytery of the James authorize a non-profit foundation to care for the site. The following year, the National Park Service placed Polegreen Church on the National Register of Historic Place. In 1995, the Historic Polegreen Foundation erected a white steel-frame replica of the church, which now serves as a memorial to religious freedom.

The remains of Confederate earthworks at Polegreen Church (DD/PG)

→ TO THE FIRST SHILOH BAPTIST CHURCH (STOP 6)

Make a left out of the parking lot and another left onto Rural Point Road. In one half mile, turn left onto Pole Green Road (this is a busy road so please proceed with caution). In 1.8 miles, turn right onto Walnut Grove Road. The battle of Bethesda Church, which is depicted by a Virginia historical marker on the Mechanicsville Turnpike, was fought in this area. You will travel back across the Mechanicsville Turnpike. Shortly thereafter, the First Shiloh Baptist Church will be on your left. Please exercise discretion around the area as the Turnpike is heavily and speedily traveled.

In 1924, a monument was erected to commemorate the men of the 36th Wisconsin Infantry during the action of June 1, 1864. Today, the monument stands on the edge of a field alongside Pole Green Road near a private residence. Please exercise extreme caution if you plan to visit, as there is no immediate pull-off. (PG)

The Battle of Bethesda Church

CHAPTER FIVE

MAY 29-30, 1864

What had become commonplace during the Overland Campaign when the armies were entrenched within close proximity to each other happened again along the Totopotomoy Creek: small skirmishes erupted along the line on and off all day. That changed drastically on the morning of May 30. "In accordance with orders from General Lee, I moved to the right," wrote Jubal Early, tasked with striking the Union left flank. "At this point [Bethesda Church], the enemy was encountered."

Early's sally forth would temporarily disrupt Union movements and sharply interrupt the routine of action along the Totopotomoy.

The morning of May 29 found many a tired Union soldier resting on the south bank of the Pamunkey. In the camps of the V Corps, Gouverneur Warren prepared to launch a reconnaissance. For the mission, he chose the division of Brig. Gen. Charles Griffin. "Hundreds . . . could be seen . . . wending their way . . . with blistered bare feet, unable to wear shoes, caused by wading the streams and marching over sand and stones," wrote one soldier from Griffin's division. Sore feet aside, it was time to find the Rebels.

The division moved out before eight, halting briefly before continuing. Unlike Hancock, Griffin was able to get across the meandering Totopotomoy Creek and advance along Shady Grove Road before

Nothing remains of the Bethesda Church battlefield, which has been lost to development. (CM)

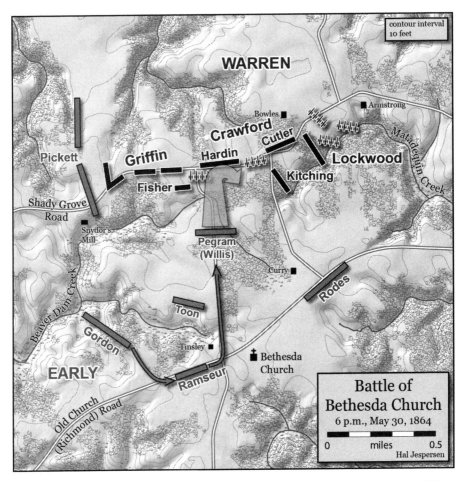

BATTLE OF BETHESDA CHURCH—The battle of Bethesda Church on May 30, 1864, pitted Jubal Early and the Second Corps of the Army of Northern Virginia against the V Corps under Gouverneur Warren. Although spirited, Early's attack faltered.

running into Confederate skirmishers. Sporadic firing continued throughout the remainder of the day.

Griffin's men were able to brush aside the Rebel pickets and the advance along Shady Grove Road continued the next morning. Warren's march was to help facilitate the arrival of Maj. Gen. Ambrose Burnside's IX Corps. Essentially, Warren was to act as a moving hinge to allow Burnside to close the door on a gap that existed between himself and Hancock. Griffin again led the way but was harassed through much of the day by enemy skirmishers who attempted to impede the advance.

While Griffin and Burnside labored into

position, Lee had settled on a course of action to find and turn the Union flank. Marse Robert was gambling again, willing to send one corps—Early's—around the flank while another, Anderson's, would support the attack and be on hand to exploit any breach in the Union line. The result would be the name of another small Virginia hamlet etched into the stitching of battle flags and the typeface of newspapers printing casualty reports.

Early in the afternoon, Warren directed his Third Division, under the command of Brig. Gen. Samuel Crawford, to move into line on Griffin's left. The bulk of Crawford's division consisted of two brigades of Pennsylvania Reserves, commanded by Cols. Martin Hardin and Joseph Fisher. These soldiers had been accepted into service by the Commonwealth of Pennsylvania at the war's outset after the state had met is required Federal quota. Incredibly, the men were set to be mustered out of the army the very next day—May 31. A soldier in the ranks of the Reserves wrote that it would be the parting of "those who had shared the last cracker, who had slept under the same blanket, who had picketed together through many weary hours . . . and who had stood side by side when the storm of death was sweeping by." Augmenting Crawford

"[R]egiments opened a furious fire, pouring volley after volley of musketry upon the advancing line . . . ." (B&L)

The last fight of the Pennsylvania Reserves (LOC)

Brig. Gen. Samuel Crawford, who had been a surgeon before the war, commanded the division that consisted largely of the Pennsylvania Reserves. (LOC)

were the 6th and 15th New York Heavy Artillery, commanded by Col. J. Howard Kitching.

Crawford dispatched Col. Martin Hardin's brigade south to Old Church Road. This thoroughfare rested some three quarters of a mile south of Shady Grove Road. Uncovered, it offered a prime axis of advance for an enemy force onto the V Corps' flank and, ultimately, the army's rear. Kitching's regiments followed in support.

Hardin emerged on Old Church Road near a local house of worship known as Bethesda Church. He immediately sent "forward a strong skirmish line." It was not long before the Pennsylvanians came scurrying back ahead a solid line of gray infantry—the Second Corps of the Army of Northern Virginia.

Early's corps had begun its movement toward the rendezvous at Bethesda Church sometime in the early afternoon. By 2:00 p.m. Maj. Gen. Robert Rodes, in command of a Second Corps division, began heading out the Old Church Road, having come overland from the Shady Grove Road. Following the Virginian was Brig. Gen. Stephen Ramseur's division. A final division under the mercurial Georgian Maj. Gen. John Gordon would be held in reserve, ready to pounce when needed to exploit gains made by the first two divisions.

As chance would have it, Early was in a great position. He had two veteran divisions ready to advance on the unsuspecting Union brigades guarding the Union flank at Bethesda Church.

Spearheading the assault was Brig. Gen. Bryan Grimes' North Carolinians, whose quick movement chased the Union skirmishers back to the main

"The Bucktail's Last Shot" by Alfred Waud. The Bucktails were part of the Pennsylvania Reserves. (LOC)

line and overpowered Hardin's brigade. The Reserves collapsed beneath the Rebel onslaught, and Hardin's men began a withdrawal back to Shady Grove Road. Kitching fared just as poorly as Hardin. One member of the 15th New York Heavy Artillery recalled plainly that they were "obliged to retire . . . the enemy making a general attack."

Waiting for Hardin's and Kitching's retreating soldiers was Warren. Reacting to the eruption of gunfire on his left flank led him to galvanize a makeshift defense along Shady Grove Road. The Union line resembled a half-moon. Kitching and Hardin reformed on the left and center, respectively, while Fisher held the right. The Yankees began to throw up earthworks and awaited the assault they knew was coming.

Following Grimes' Tar Heels came Brig. Gen. John Pegram's Virginia Brigade, led that day by Col. Edward Willis. The Virginians unsuspectingly ran into the half-moon shaped Union entrenchments. The ensuing assault never stood a chance against the prepared defenses.

"About twenty five yards in front of the . . . rifle pits was a fence and some bushes that concealed our pits and men from view," a soldier in the 2nd Pennsylvania Reserves described. "The enemy advanced to the fence in most excellent order, and as they reached it, our whole line, which had not fired a shot, opened upon them a crushing fire of musketry, while the artillery poured in canister and . . . shells." Another man recalled the Federal "regiments opened a furious fire, pouring volley after volley of musketry upon the advancing line . . . the enemy's column was broken and driven back."

Maj. Gen. Richard Anderson assumed command of the Confederate First Corps after former commander James Longstreet was accidentally wounded by his own men in the Wilderness. (LOC)

Lee's "Bad Old Man," Maj. Gen. Jubal Early, assumed command of the Confederate Second Corps after former commander Richard Ewell fell ill following the engagement along the North Anna River. (LOC)

Early had sent Pegram's brigade forward, he later recounted, "with one of Rodes' brigades on its right, to feel the enemy, and ascertain his strength." What the Virginians found was a formidable Union defense—and more than 200 of them fell in finding that answer. Included in that number was the acting brigade commander, Willis, who was mortally wounded, and two regimental commanders who were killed outright.

"Never was a more gallant charge made," a surviving Union soldier said of the charge.

As blood was shed north of the forlorn church, Anderson's commitment was half-hearted. Per Lee's instructions, Anderson had shifted to cover Early's departure. He had sent one division, under Maj. Gen. George Pickett, out Shady Grove Church Road toward Griffin's division. Reaching the Union position, Pickett summed up the situation and decided to not attack fortified Union positions, possibly haunted by the memories of the previous summer.

With that, Anderson's role in the fighting was over.

The day ended with a readjustment of both lines to incorporate the movement of the day. A promising flank attack and battle plan had gone awry. For Lee and his army, the casualties that he could not afford had marked the failure. Maybe there was something in the water or in the air east of Richmond that sapped Confederate commanders of their enterprising spirit. Two years earlier, in 1862, it had been Stonewall Jackson that had hesitated at White Oak Swamp. On May 30, 1864, it was Anderson at Bethesda Church.

With one day left in that bloody May, the two armies would look toward another Virginia hamlet—a small crossroads called Cold Harbor.

At First Shiloh Baptist Church

Similar to the Confederate lines along Totopotomoy Creek, much of the Bethesda Church battlefield has been consumed by development. As

First Shiloh Baptist Church (PG)

you park at the Shiloh Baptist Church and take in the area that was the battlefield, traffic will zoom by along the Mechanicsville Turnpike. Even in 1864, the area around Bethesda Church, like much of this portion of the eastern suburbs of Virginia, was crucial for transportation. Control of points such as the intersection ahead would allow one side to protect their flank; failure to guard diligently and completely could lead to an opportunity for the other side.

Guarding Warren's flank and Old Church Road was normally relegated for cavalry. Following the battle at Haw's Shop, though, Sheridan had withdrawn his divisions to the vicinity of Old Church. Warren had requested his services; however, as with Meade, Sheridan had an icy relationship with the V Corps commander as a result of the botched march to Spotsylvania. Sheridan remained at Old Church to guard the approaches to White House Landing and await the arrival of Smith's XVIII Corps. Protection of Warren's flank instead fell to the brigade of Col. Martin Hardin.

Bethesda Church itself stood to your immediate right front, near the brick wall and just southeast of the intersection of Walnut Grove Road and

The Mechanicsville Pike can be so busy that it can be hard even to read the state historical marker along the roadside—the only testament to the fighting that once took place there. (CM)

Old Church Road (modern Mechanicsville Turnpike). Incredibly, the building survived the battle only to burn down three years after the war ended. Reaching this position in the middle of the afternoon of May 30, Hardin sent the 1st and 13th Pennsylvania Reserves west on a reconnaissance. The two regiments ran into a brigade of North Carolinian infantry commanded by Brig. Gen. Bryan Grimes and were quickly overwhelmed. The Tar Heels pushed the Pennsylvanians back toward the church, and Hardin retreated north along Walnut Grove Road.

Later in the day, Jubal Early used this area as a jumping off point for his assault against Warren's line along Shady Grove Road (modern-day Pole Green Road). Early, known as "Lee's Bad Old Man," was an irascible 44-year-old bachelor in 1864. He was placed in charge of the Second Corps because of his dependable service and his aggressive offensive-mindedness. The Second Corps, Stonewall Jackson's old command, had been hard hit at Spotsylvania Court House but still had some of the best troops in Lee's army.

Bethesda Church marked the last hurrah for the Pennsylvania Reserves. They had fought their first battle almost two years earlier—on June 26, 1862—at nearby Beaver Dam Creek. Now, on the morning of June 1—the day after their tussle with the Second Corps at Bethesda Church—their

Battlefield Park Elementary School sits near the site once occupied by Bethesda Church. (CM)

enlistments expired and the Reserves were mustered out of Federal service. Perhaps because of their devotion to each other and the Union cause, over 1,700 men in the ranks decided to re-enlist. They were organized into two new regiments, the 190th and 191st Pennsylvania Infantry.

⟶ TO THE LOCATION OF THE CAVALRY ACTION (STOP 7)

Turn left out of the parking lot and proceed 0.8 miles on Walnut Grove Road. Turn left onto Colts Neck Road (Rt. 633) and proceed 0.7 miles and make another left onto Sandy Valley Road (Rt. 635). In one half mile, turn right onto Beulah Church Road (Rt. 633). After approximately 1.5 miles, turn left onto Crown Hill Road (Rt. 632) and in 0.8 miles you will see a stone sign reading "Madison Estates." Make the left there and then a very quick left into a small paved parking lot. In front of you will be the Virginia historical marker for Stop 7.

Another Crossroads

CHAPTER SIX

MAY 31, 1864

Grant was up before sunrise on the morning of May 31. His headquarters was a little less than two miles west of Haw's Shop in a clearing north of Shady Grove Road. Grant's first task after lighting a cigar was to send a dispatch back to Washington. Simple and concise, Grant wrote that Warren had repulsed Early the evening before with "considerable slaughter." One of Grant's staff officers remembered how he was beginning to turn his attention to the south, beyond the army's left flank.

While he was still engaged along the North Anna, Grant ordered Maj. Gen. Benjamin Butler to send Maj. Gen. William Smith's XVIII Corps from the Army of the James to reinforce the Army of the Potomac. Butler's spring offensive had been ground to a halt at Bermuda Hundred below Richmond, and Grant felt that the men could better serve elsewhere. Smith's men sailed down the James River, entered the York River, and then moved up the Pamunkey. As both sides lurched toward their collision at Bethesda Church, Smith was disembarking at the Yankees' main supply base at White House Landing. However, Confederate cavalry had moved up between the Potomac army and White House the previous day to assail Phil Sheridan at Old Church. The enemy presence had the potential to cause headaches for Smith's imminent arrival.

Federal cavalry pushed along this road to open the way to Cold Harbor, continuing to demonstrate dominance over their Confederate counterparts. (DD/PG)

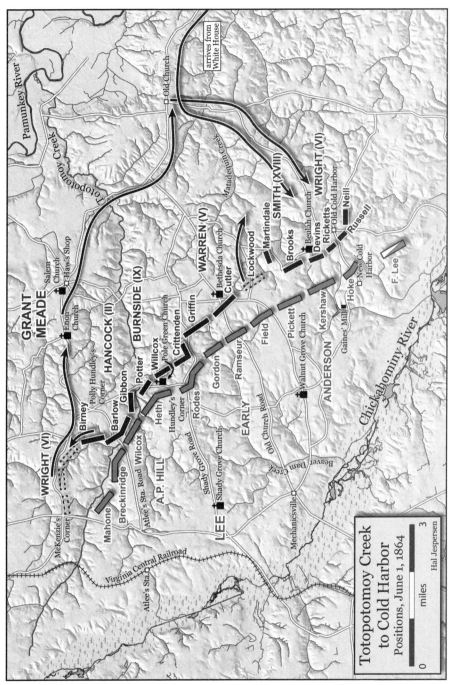

TOTOPOTOMOY CREEK TO COLD HARBOR—Continuing with the trend that had developed during the course of the Overland Campaign, both sides dug extensive and intricate fortifications on both sides of Totopotomoy Creek. Seeing no advantage, Grant decided to sidle around Lee's right flank again, which led blue-clad forces toward Cold Harbor.

For the South, the need for reinforcements was paramount. A dire tone seeped into communications between Lee, Confederate President Jefferson Davis, and Gen. Pierre Gustave Toutant Beauregard— the one-time hero of First Manassas and now the Confederate commander at Petersburg, who was the only possible source of reinforcements. Beauregard resisted, stating his need for troops to continue to defend Petersburg, keep the Union force at Bermuda Hundred bottled, and keep open the lines of communication and supplies running south and west from Petersburg. Lee, however, saw the bigger picture and stated bluntly: "If this army is unable to resist Grant, the troops under . . . Beauregard and in the city will be unable to defend it."

Lee, desperate for reinforcements, got them in the form of Maj. Gen. Robert Hoke's division, transferred north from Beauregard's forces south of the James River. (LOC)

Furthermore, with Grant receiving the XVIII Corps, Lee again warned that troops had to be reassigned to him from Petersburg so he could counter. If not, he once again predicted, "the result of this delay would be disaster."

Beauregard took heed of Lee's pleas for help and sent Maj. Gen. Robert Hoke's division north. Led by the brigade of Brig. Gen. Thomas Clingman, they would start toward Lee's army the next day, May 31. Unbeknownst to the North Carolinian at the time, their presence would be greatly needed.

The "Gray Fox" in command of the Army of Northern Virginia already had a plan for these new arrivals—much like the cavalry reinforcements at Haw's Shop earlier in the campaign. He intended to send them to a road junction known as Old Cold Harbor. Occupation of this vital crossroads was critical in protecting the army's right flank and the approach to Richmond.

Otherwise, even after the repulse at Bethesda Church, Lee's army still retained a strong defensive line on the south bank of the Totopotomoy. The Second Corps, which had borne the brunt of the Bethesda Church action, had taken up position approximately a mile to the west of that battleground. With Early's men in this position, Lee and his army covered more than eight miles, with one flank guarding the vital Virginia Central

Railroad and the opposite anchored on the Old Church Road.

Lee's Northern counterparts were not stationary during this time. Sheridan's troopers advanced following their fight at Old Church. Toward the middle of the afternoon, Sheridan, ever the aggressor, decided to send Brig. Gen. Alfred Torbert's division against the Confederate cavalry, now in position around the Old Cold Harbor crossroads. Torbert planned to send his brigades in tandem along separate roads and hoped that Brig. Gens. Wesley Merritt and George Custer would hold the Rebels in place long enough for Col. Thomas Devin, known as "Buford's Hard Hitter," to turn the enemy right. Torbert wrote that the assault was "an excellent opportunity to strike the enemy a severe blow."

Union soldiers at Cold Harbor
(LOC)

Picketing the approach to Old Cold Harbor was Gen. Fitzhugh Lee's cavalrymen, who'd been sent to bolster two overmatched cavalry brigades. As the Yankees moved on Cold Harbor Road, they ran into one of Lee's brigades, commanded by Brig. Gen. Lunsford Lomax. Merritt, leading the advance, wrote that his men drove back Lomax "without much loss" to "the immediate vicinity of the cross-roads." The Union troopers found that the Confederates "had thrown up temporary breast-works, consisting of rails, logs and earth." There, the Rebels "poured a heavy fire" into Merritt's ranks.

Arriving to assist the cavalry was Clingman's Brigade from Hoke's division, which took up a position on Lomax's left. Together with Brig. Gen. William Wickham's brigade, these troops tried in desperation to stop Sheridan's momentum.

Meanwhile, over on Merritt's left, Devin's advance was also slowed by impediments in the road. His troopers encountered enemy pickets from Wickham's brigade behind "a barricade with dense thickets on each side." Devin recalled, "The nature of the country effectually prevented a mounted command from reaching the right flank of the enemy's position."

Col. Thomas Devin had earned his nickname, "Buford's Hard Hitter," during his service under former cavalry commander Brig. Gen. John Buford. Buford died of typhoid in December of 1863, but Devin continued on as a cavalryman—and continued to hit hard. The nickname stuck.
(LOC)

The action swayed through the late afternoon hours. Despite having to leave a regiment at Bermuda Hundred, the 8th, 31st, and 51st North Carolina of Clingman's brigade held their own against the Union cavalry. The Fifty-First even advanced about a half mile in front of their comrades to the "most exposed" portion of the line.

Cavalry at Old Church (LOC)

As the day dragged on, Merritt resolved to do what Devin could not. With the additional weight of Custer's regiments, Merritt launched an assault on the enemy's left. Hitting home, the attack overwhelmed the North Carolinians. With Clingman's line compromised, the rest of the Confederate position became untenable. The Rebels hastily abandoned their position, leaving the Old Cold Harbor crossroads in the hands of the victorious Union troopers.

Sheridan sent a message summarizing the fight back to headquarters and also relayed the fact that he had encountered gray infantry. Probably feeling isolated and facing overwhelming numbers, Little Phil declared that he would not be able to hold his position. Incredibly, the Confederates did not even realize the Union horsemen had slinked away into the night.

Sheridan's dispatch sent waves through army headquarters. An examination of a map revealed that one of the roads that passed through Cold Harbor was extremely important. Travelling east would lead one to White House Landing and Smith's XVIII Corps. To the west lay the Chickahominy River and Richmond. Clearly, the initiative would lay with whichever side could hold the road junction. Meade immediately sent a courier galloping back to Sheridan, instructing him to remain in place.

A decision was also made to send Maj. Gen. Horatio Wright's VI Corps that night to Sheridan's assistance. After crossing the Pamunkey, these veterans had marched to Hanover Court House

Promoted to brigadier general in June 1863, Merritt served alternately as a brigade and interim division commander during the Overland Campaign and would ultimately succeed Sheridan as commander of the Cavalry Corps. (LOC)

before taking up a position on the right of the II Corps. Unlike Hancock and Warren, Wright had seen little fighting since the battle of Spotsylvania Court House. Additionally, his position on the northern end of the line made it easier for him to disengage. Late that night, Meade ordered Wright to march on the crossroads.

Finally Grant and Meade had a clear purpose. For the last three days, they had danced with Lee along the Totopotomoy and at Bethesda Church. Control of Cold Harbor could very well decide the campaign.

Cold Harbor, a seemingly innocuous crossroads in the Tidewater of Virginia, was the latest key to unlocking potential victory for Grant. Would Lee be able to keep the door closed again?

At The Site of the Cavalry Fighting

Interestingly, there are two Cold Harbor crossroads: Old Cold Harbor and New Cold Harbor. Neither refer to a conventional type of "harbor," though. Old Cold Harbor, which held so much importance to both sides, consisted only of a tavern. Inferring from its name, the tavern may not have been fully operational—it didn't serve hot meals. The term "cold harbours," then, often indicated a roadside dwelling where travelers could stay only overnight and had to provide their own resources. Situated just a few miles west of Old Cold Harbor, on the Gaines Mill battlefield, was

New Cold Harbor tavern (B&L)

the crossroads of New Cold Harbor. The battle of Gaines Mill, fought on June 27, 1862, was one of the bloodiest days in American history: more than 18,000 men fell that day. Only 5,000 more fell at Antietam later that same year. Now, two years later, the armies had come back to this same area.

Both battlefields, preserved and administered by the National Park Service, offer excellent trail networks, with interpretive markers, to guide you around the fields of fury. One can peer over the still-snaking, looping earthen mounds (but please do not climb on the earthworks) and see the open fields at

Old Cold Harbor tavern (NPS)

Cold Harbor. Or make your way over to Gaines Mill and see the incline and swampy bottomlands attacking Confederate soldiers had to muck across to reach the source of the whizzing iron balls and exploding, ripping shards of cannon shots in the early summer of 1862.

The ground on each side of Cold Harbor Road (modern Crown Hill Road) was hotly contested by Union and Confederate cavalry on May 31, 1864. Stymied by a stiff Confederate defense, Wesley Merritt decided to send the 1st and 2nd U.S. Cavalry, along with the 5th Michigan Cavalry, off to your right to turn the Confederate line.

The Old Cold Harbor tavern intersection sits 1.3 miles to the northeast of the location where New Cold Harbor tavern sat. Today, a triangle of roads converge there. None of the buildings are of the Civil War era, although a pair of historical markers outlines some of the action that took place there during the Penninsula Campaign. (CM)

During the 1862 battle of
Gaines Mill, Federals held
this ridge overlooking
Boatswain's Creek. (DD)

Observing the progress of Merritt's flank attack, George Custer ordered Maj. Melvin Brewer of the 1st Michigan Cavalry to launch a mounted charge down the road against the enemy line in front of you. The combined attacks were successful and the Confederates were driven from the field.

The cavalry fight around the Old Cold Harbor crossroads on May 31 was actually a continuation of two days of sparring. Prior to the fighting at Bethesda Church, South Carolina horsemen under Brig. Gen. Matthew C. Butler attacked Sheridan's pickets near Old Church. Butler had been dispatched on a reconnaissance to determine if there was a strong Union presence beyond Lee's right flank. Just as at Haw's Shop, the Yankee troopers got the better of their counterparts. Sheridan ended up overwhelming Butler and pushing the Rebels back to Cold Harbor.

Although urban sprawl has begun to intrude on many tracts of the Cold Harbor area, there is enough rural terrain still left to get a grasp of the rolling countryside. Open fields, interspersed with woodlots, still dot the area. You can still remove yourself from the hustle and bustle and appreciate the quietness of the landscape; you can still make yourself hear the neighing of horses, the clatter of swords and scabbards against legs, and the shout of orders being passed down the ranks. Imagine the desperation of the Confederates under Butler,

grudgingly giving way against the confident and aggressive Union cavalry. Although outnumbered, if the gray-clad horsemen could hold on, infantry support was on the way.

Later that night, when the infantry did arrive, the confusion of the same dark, moonless fields and shadowy forests would mask the retrograde movement of the Union cavalry.

Federal cavalry charged across this field, in the direction of Cold Harbor, to clear away Confederate resistance. (PG)

➡ TO THE COLD HARBOR BATTLEFIELD VISITOR CENTER (STOP 8)

Make the right out of the small paved parking lot and then make another quick right back onto Crown Hill Road. In approximately one mile, you will continue onto Cold Harbor Road. The Cold Harbor Battlefield Visitor Center will be on your right, after the street name change, in approximately one half mile.

"A Hurricane from the Heavens"

CHAPTER SEVEN
JUNE 1, 1864

A pale, early summer moon shone down on the VI Corps as they trudged along the Virginia byroads toward Cold Harbor. One soldier recalled "the march was a hard one . . . . The dust, ankle deep, raised in clouds by the column, was . . . suffocating. It filled the air and hung upon the leaves of the trees like snow. Seldom had our men experienced so severe a march."

Major General Horatio Wright had been in command of these hardened soldiers for less than a month. He had taken over for the beloved Maj. Gen. John Sedgwick, who fell at the battle of Spotsylvania Court House. "Uncle John" had been killed on May 9 after deriding enemy sharpshooters by saying "they could not hit an elephant at this range." Wright's conduct would be critical if the Federals wished to retain control of the crossroads.

Ahead of them, Torbert's cavalry brigades had returned to their old positions after Sheridan received Meade's missive. The cavalrymen anxiously awaited the Rebel effort to recapture the intersection. "The works were reconstructed . . . and were of incalculable value," a trooper from the 9th New York Cavalry wrote afterwards. "The troops . . . were placed along this line, boxes of ammunition distributed and orders given that the line must hold."

That line would be tested by Confederate

A monument on the Cold Harbor National Battlefield commemorates the first engagement of the 2nd Connecticut Heavy Artillery. (CM)

infantry, many of whom had spent the night getting into position. One of Hoke's brigades had tussled with the Union cavalry the day before, but now he had the rest of his division on hand for the forthcoming brawl. Coming over from the First Corps to support him was the veteran division of Maj. Gen. Joseph Kershaw.

Anderson's orders were to launch a two-pronged assault. Kershaw would begin the action with an advance in the direction of Beulah Church. When his division stepped off, he was to notify Hoke. After receiving word, the North Carolinian would send his division toward Old Cold Harbor. Major Generals George Pickett and Charles Field—commanders of the other two First Corps divisions—would be on hand to provide support when a breakthrough occurred.

Around daybreak, Kershaw launched his attack. One unique characteristic of the attack was by the brigade of Col. Laurence M. Keitt, formerly Kershaw's old command. Keitt had just arrived with the 20th South Carolina from garrison duty in Charleston and reported to Kershaw's division in late May. The other South Carolina regiments in the division, all veterans, were shocked to see the sheer number of men the 20th brought to the field—approximately 1,100 men total. That was the size of Kershaw's entire brigade, which showed just how much the war had attrited their own numbers by 1864. Keitt shocked the South Carolinians even further by preparing to lead the charge while sitting atop a horse in front of the command—yet another reminder of the earlier, and more naive, days of the war.

Major James Kidd of the 6th Michigan Cavalry remembered, "General Custer ordered all the . . . artillery to fire with shell and canister which they did most effectively." Custer wrote later that "heavy firing was kept up for a long time, but the enemy finding our position too strong, withdrew."

"Withdrew" was putting it mildly. The Confederate attack had barely begun when Keitt, on his horse, went down with a mortal wound shortly after the command entered the woods that masked the Union lines. His attack faltered quickly thereafter in front of the amazing firepower of Torbert's Spencer-carbine-wielding cavalrymen.

The various regimental commanders tried to communicate an orderly withdrawal to the Bethesda Church Road—at least that was the plan, but what happened next was exactly the opposite. According to an artilleryman present, he had "never seen any body of troops in such a condition of utter demoralization."

With this repulse, the rest of Kershaw's division, stacked up in the road waiting to enter the fray, did what had become commonplace during the campaign: entrench. Hoke, waiting patiently to advance when the order and noise of the assault reached him, finally received word that Kershaw's advance had failed.

Maj. Gen. Horatio Wright had taken over command of the Union VI Corps after beloved commander "Uncle John" Sedgwick was killed at Spotsylvania on May 9. (LOC)

The blue-clad cavalrymen had performed ably. Around 10 a.m., the lead elements of the VI corps began to arrive at Cold Harbor and relieve their mounted comrades. Wright received orders to attack as soon as possible. With his columns strung out behind him, it would be several hours before his men would be on line and ready to make the assault. Joining the VI Corps in their coming assault would be Smith's XVIII Corps. Augmenting Smith was another division from the X Corps of the Army of the James under Brig. Gen. Charles Devens. Botched instructions had mistakenly directed Smith to march from White House Landing to the Union line along the Totopotomoy, rather than to Cold Harbor. After exchanging messages with headquarters, the directions were adjusted and the wandering division made its way to the field.

Maj. Gen. William "Baldy" Smith, commander of the Union XVIII Corps, was not actually bald. Although he accrused a respectable record on the battlefield, he also had a reputation for being a headache for his seniors. (LOC)

Throughout the morning and into the afternoon, Wright's soldiers filed into line just west of Cold Harbor. Brigadier General Thomas Neill's division held the southern end of the line. On Neill's right, Brig. Gen. David Russell continued the line to the Cold Harbor Road. North of the road and forming on Russell's right was the division of Brig. Gen. James Ricketts. Smith arrived to deploy on Ricketts' right and extend the Union line. The

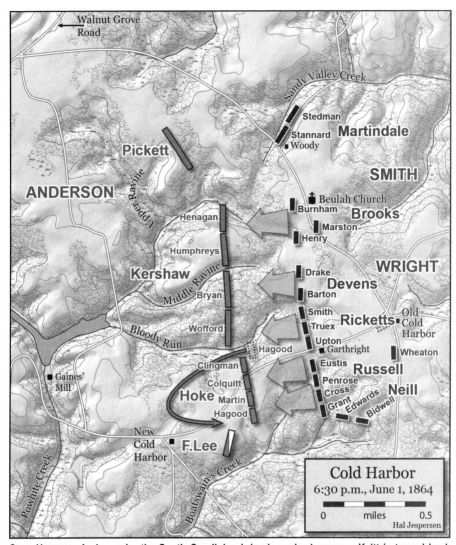

COLD HARBOR—A charge by the South Carolinian brigade under Lawrence Keitt is turned back early in the day. The brigade will reform under John Henagan. This ushers in a day of fighting. The attack of the Union VI Corps under Horatio Wright slams into the Confederate divisions of Joseph Kershaw and Robert Hoke later in the evening, although the Federals gain little headway.

divisions of Brig. Gens. Charles Devens, William T. H. "Bully" Brooks, and John Martindale, respectively, deployed on Ricketts' right.

Anderson's failure to capture Cold Harbor forced Lee to send additional men to counter the Union buildup off his right flank. Major General Breckenridge was ordered midmorning to head toward Cold Harbor. The Rebel concentration soon began to rival that of Smith and Wright.

Hoke's division made up the far right of the line, with Kershaw, Pickett, and Field filing in on his left.

As the VI and XVIII corps came on line, the Confederates, situated about a mile and a half away, had used their time wisely to construct and improve their position. Whenever the Union attack came, they would be ready.

At 6 p.m. the Federal line rolled forward. Advancing along the Cold Harbor Road was Brig. Gen. Emory Upton's brigade. A surgeon in one of his regiments recalled that Upton was acting particularly "wolfish" that day. Leading Upton's assault was the 2nd Connecticut Heavy Artillery.

Wright's VI Corps attacked at 6 p.m. with some success. (LOC)

In preparing for the attack, Upton decided to use the same tactics that had worked so well for him at Spotsylvania. The feisty brigade commander instructed the regiment's colonel, Elisha Kellogg, to form his regiment in three lines. The first line was to move forward against the Rebel works as rapidly as possible and, if luck held, breach the enemy position. The two succeeding lines of Connecticut soldiers would move up and exploit the breach. As they crossed the open field toward the enemy works, at no point were the New Englanders to stop and return fire as they made their charge.

Upton wrote that the regiment "moved to the assault in beautiful order. Crossing an open field, it entered a pine-wood, passed down a gentle declivity and up a slight ascent . . . . For seventy feet in front of the works the trees had been felled, interlocking with each other and barring all further advance . . . . Up to these, to the foot of the works, the brave men rushed."

During the Union assault on June 1, Emory Upton's brigade moved across this ground to strike the Confederate line. (DD/PG)

A soldier sketch mis-titled "Battle of Coal Harbor" shows the 122nd New York, advancing past the Garthright House, during the June 1 attack. (HCP&R)

"Here they come," the butternut defenders called to one another—a now-common refrain in the campaign.

Brigadier General Clingman, in charge of the defense, wrote later about the advance of the 2nd Connecticut. "They showed probably about thirty men in front and were closed in mass very compactly," he described. "They had on apparently new uniforms and were marching at quick-step." The first enemy volley was high and passed over the heads of the men in the lead. Clingman yelled to his men, "aim low and aim well." Their fire was telling. It crashed into the Federal ranks, one Connecticut officer remembered, like "a hurricane from the heavens."

Two hundred and fifty men crumpled. The volleys broke the Union advance. Kellogg attempted to withdraw but was shot down.

Into this maelstrom rode Upton. The young brigadier dismounted his wounded horse and promptly began shouting instructions in an effort to restore order. His presence helped to calm the men. One soldier remembered that Upton was the "coolest man I ever saw in the hottest of the fight." At one point, Upton grabbed a musket and took cover behind a tree. Each time he fired, he would pass the empty weapon back to the men behind him for a loaded one.

THE CONFEDERATE VOLLEYS CRASHED INTO THE FEDERAL RANKS . . . LIKE "A HURRICANE FROM THE HEAVENS."

"The storm of battle seemed suddenly to have broken," a soldier in the 77th New York recalled. "The whole line thundered with the incessant volleys of musketry, and the shot and shell of the artillery shrieked and howled like spirits of evil . . . . The clouds of dust and smoke almost obscured the terrible scene."

The XVIII Corps moved in concert with Wright. "The ground occupied . . . was covered with thick wood and intersected by ravines. It was likewise in close proximity to the rifle pits of the enemy, from which a murderous fire was kept up on my entire line," recalled Brig. Gen. Gilman Marston, commanding one of Smith's brigades. "The casualties . . . were very large."

From this position, Confederate riflemen cut down the attacking VI Corps divisions late on June 1. (DD/PG)

This began a seesaw fight as the Confederate force staggered under the blows delivered against it. To stem the tide in front of Kershaw and Hoke, Anderson countered by pulling various brigades from Field's division, which was not engaged, but it wasn't enough. Despite the stiff resistance, Wright and Smith forced the Rebels out of their first line of works.

Once their assault sputtered out, Federals began to entrench. (B&L)

The fighting began to dissipate around dusk. Without reserves to exploit their success, the Federals could do little but dig in and solidify their lines. Their newly occupied position would be the jumping off point for their next assault.

In some instances, only 50 yards separated the men wearing the blue from those wearing the gray. It would not be long before thousands of men would fall either defending or trying to conquer those 50 yards.

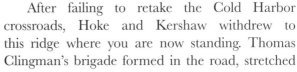

At The Cold Harbor Visitor Center

After failing to retake the Cold Harbor crossroads, Hoke and Kershaw withdrew to this ridge where you are now standing. Thomas Clingman's brigade formed in the road, stretched to the north and bent back to guard the reaches of the ravines to your immediate left front. This position became the epicenter of the Confederate line as Lee sent more troops into this area. The driving tour and walking trail will take you through the fighting that took place here from June 1 to June 3.

The implementation of fieldworks over the course of the Overland Campaign represented a tactical evolution by the Rebels; the Federals needed to evolve, too, if they hoped to dislodge them from their battlements. The Union army had yet to confront defenses of this magnitude before, and it would take a special innovation to counteract the ingenuity of their enemy. It would come from a fiery colonel from New York, Emory Upton.

Emory Upton was a West Point graduate and commanded a brigade in the VI Corps. At Spotsylvania, Upton was quick to recognize that the changes made by the Confederates outmatched the traditional Napoleonic tactics employed by Union army. Assaults utilizing two lines of men in close order would be chewed apart by the Rebels. So, Upton proposed a revolutionary idea of his own: rather than attacking in the old style, the Union soldiers would attack in column. Massed in a larger, tighter formation, they would advance against the enemy entrenchments as quickly as possible without stopping to fire. The sheer force of the concentrated forward movement would then allow the Federals to punch a hole in the enemy line. However, for the assault to be completely successful, supporting troops were necessary to move up and exploit the breach created by the column formation.

The Federal attack on June 1 drove Confederates back to a ridge where the National Park Service Visitor Center now stands. There, the Confederates held. Today, cannon mark the approximate spot once occupied by the four-gun battery of the Richmond Fayette Artillery—part of Maj. J. P. W. Read's battalion—which supported the Georgia brigade of Brig. Gen. Alfred Colquitt. (CM)

On May 10, Upton was given 12 regiments for an assault on the northwestern section of the "Mule Shoe." Assembling in a three by four formation, the Union wedge tore open a massive gap in the Confederate line. "The assault was a complete success," Upton wrote. "We went over two lines of formidable entrenchments . . . . Had fresh troops . . . been at hand the enemy must have been badly beaten."

Although Upton was eventually driven back, the assault brought him a promotion to brigadier general. Grant was so impressed that two days later he sent Winfield Scott Hancock's entire II Corps, twenty thousand men, against the tip of the salient. Once again, the Federals enjoyed initial success. Unfortunately, supports did not arrive in time, allowing the Confederates to counterattack and seal the gap.

Upton would employ the same tactics used at Spotsylvania in the assault with the 2nd Connecticut Heavy Artillery at Cold Harbor.

Upton's attack against the Muleshoe Salient on May 10 sent hundreds of Confederate prisoners streaming to the rear. (LOC)

Emory Upton earned his brigadier stars for the innovative tactics he developed and implemented at Spotsylvania—used again at Cold Harbor. (LOC)

→ TO COLD HARBOR BATTLEFIELD PARK (STOP 9)

Make a left out of the visitor center parking lot and proceed one-tenth of a mile and you will see on your right the sign for the Cold Harbor Park. The parking lot will be on your left after the turn. Before you turn into the lot, notice the brick-and-frame house ahead on the gravel road.

Eye of the Storm

CHAPTER EIGHT

JUNE 2, 1864

Two words could describe the night of June 1 for the foot soldiers of both armies: "slow" and "wearisome." If two words could describe the night from the commanding officers of the armies, they would be "essential" and "pivotal." Still, two more words would describe what was happening after dark on June 1: "night march."

Both Grant and Lee had by now recognized that the epicenter of operations had shifted from the Totopotomoy to Cold Harbor. Whoever could mass their troops there the quickest would likely gain the upper hand in the next round of fighting.

With the two armies in such close proximity, Confederate lookouts began to notice when Grant began shifting men to his left. Lee responded quickly. At midnight, Major General Breckenridge and his division began their march south. Lee needed Breckinridge to be at Cold Harbor by dawn to support the growing number of Confederates already opposing Wright and Smith.

As June 2 dawned, Lee decided that he needed to bolster his right flank even further. The Third Corps divisions of Maj. Gens. William Mahone and Cadmus Wilcox would follow in Breckinridge's wake and then anchor the Confederate line on the Chickahominy River.

Inevitable delays caused Breckenridge to arrive late. However, luck was on the Rebel side that day:

One of the monuments that sits next to Cold Harbor Road, on ground traversed by Union soldiers during their assaults. (DD/PG)

Maj. Gen. William Mahone, commanding a division in A.P. Hill's Third Corps, stood approximately 5'5" and weighed a mere 100 pounds. He was known aptly and affectionately as "Little Billy." (LOC)

Maj. Gen. Cadmus Wilcox, a native North Carolinian, had served with the Army of Northern Virginia throughout its existence. He had provided steady leadership, rising from colonel to major general. (LOC)

their Northern counterparts were experiencing frustrations of their own.

The day had actually started well for the Federal army. The tired VI Corps soldiers around the Cold Harbor were surprised early on that June 2 morning by the arrival of Winfield Scott Hancock's II Corps. Hancock had been ordered to march through the night to the crossroads. One soldier from the 28th Massachusetts Infantry described it as the "most severest" of the campaign. To compensate for Hancock's absence at the northern end of the line, Meade decided to draw Burnside's IX Corps back from Totopotomoy Creek to consolidate around Bethesda Church.

Hancock's instructions were to launch an assault as soon as he was able after uniting with Wright and Smith. Although his men were "worn out" after their "hot and dusty night march," Meade decided to postpone the assault until 5 p.m. that evening. Despite their bedraggled condition, Hancock placed Francis Barlow's and John Gibbon's divisions on Wright's left. A Pennsylvania officer remembered that his men were "extremely exhausted."

Meanwhile, Confederate reinforcements, albeit slowly, were approaching the new area of operations. As the day wore on, each side set about improving their positions and throwing up earthworks. "We la[id] . . . in the hot sun," a soldier from the 49th Pennsylvania remembered. "Our rifle pits keep the balls off, but not the sun." A Rhode Islander explained: "The sharpshooters have been at work . . . and it has been anything but pleasant. In the afternoon we had a heavy rain storm that seemed to dampen the ardor of both armies."

Perhaps the change in the weather had an effect on Grant. Observing the fatigued condition of the soldiers around Cold Harbor, he elected to cancel the 5 p.m. attack.

Instead, Grant sent new orders to Meade instructing him that the assault would take place on June 3. "The corps commanders were to select the points in their respective fronts where they would make their assaults," Grant later explained. "The move was

The Confederate line at Cold Harbor (LOC)

to commence at half past four in the morning."

Confederates already in the area used the extra time to improve upon their defenses—which, according to Brig. Gen. E. P. Alexander of the First Corps, "were mere little ditches that a calf might run over" in certain parts.

As though marching in quicksand, the butternut-and-gray soldiers from Breckenridge's units slowly made their way to the portion of the line that had been recently held by Fitzhugh Lee's cavalry. Hailed as the "Heroes of New Market," Breckenridge's men tromped up around 4 p.m. Shortly thereafter came the Third Corps reinforcements who finally cemented the Confederate line to the Chickahominy. Last to arrive was "Little Billy" Mahone's veterans, who encamped behind the Rebel line near another intersection known as New Cold Harbor. "We were on the extreme right of the army," one of Wilcox's men recorded, "the last shoulder of the ridge . . . [from the] Chickahominy."

Like pieces on a chessboard, the rearrangement of Lee's line now consisted of Early's Second Corps and one division from the Third Corps on the left. In the center were the divisions of Pickett, Field, and Kershaw. On Kershaw's right was Hoke's division, followed by Breckinridge and Wilcox. Behind Hoke, Mahone was entrenched as a reserve.

The new arrivals quickly began digging in, and one officer remarked about the soldiers being

Both sides consolidated their positions around Cold Harbor on June 2. Confederates constructed an intricate and daunting maze of earthworks from which to repel an expected Federal onslaught. (DD/PG)

"handy with the dirt . . . and soon erected stout fortifications." These fortifications, as it happened, would be the focal point of orders being cut by the Union high command across the intervening fields, woods, and gullies.

The unsettling peacefulness was soon shattered by gunfire near Bethesda Church. Lee, like a hardened boxer looking for an opportunity to throw in an unsuspecting jab, had left discretionary orders for his commander of the Second Corps. If an opportunity presented itself along the Union right flank, Jubal Early was to attack.

Late in the afternoon, Lee's "Bad Old Man," as Early was called, spied his chance. "In the afternoon of that day [June 2], Rode's division moved forward," he wrote. Followed by the divisions of Maj. Gens. John Gordon and Henry Heth—the lone Third Corps division still in that sector—Early "drove the enemy from his entrenchments." The ensuing assault caught Burnside's IX Corps by surprise.

A Union survivor remembered the initial contact as "a heavy discharge of shot and shell poured into us from the woods." After initial success,

Early's attack ran into stiffening Union resistance as the V Corps lent support. Although well designed in concept, Early could not press his advantage, and this second attack around Bethesda Church ended like the first with a reshaping of the lines and more names on the casualty lists.

From behind these works, men in gray awaited the eventual enemy attack on June 3. (DD/PG)

"In this movement there was some heavy fighting and several hundred prisoners were taken by us," Early remembered, writing afterwards. "Brigadier-General [George] Doles, a gallant officer of Rode's division, was killed, but otherwise our loss was not severe."

As the guns fell silent, except for the occasional picket firing, thousands of soldiers bedded down for the night. Many had just spent their last day on earth.

All the fighting since the crossing of the Rapidan River had led up to the third day in June. Lee had deftly thwarted the Army of the Potomac in the Wilderness, at Spotsylvania, and along the North Anna. In spite of the stunning losses the Federals had sustained thus far in the campaign, Grant had pushed Lee back upon Richmond. The city lay just 10 miles from Cold Harbor.

By June 2, Confederate and Federal forces had virtually swapped positions near Bethesda Church. (LOC)

However formidable those Confederate lines were, Grant could not ignore the chance of one great assault breaking through and opening the road to the Confederate capital. Since crossing the Pamunkey, it seemed that his fortunes were beginning to turn. The successful skirmishing at Totopotomoy Creek, the repulse of the Rebels at Bethesda Church, and the minor gains of the assaults of June 1 were encouraging, even emboldening. Grant's original objective—to wear Lee down—finally looked as if it was working. Given the events of the last week, the assault, if properly executed, could spell an end to the fighting and quite possibly, the war. Grant had to try—and with his characteristic bulldog tenacity, one could expect a great effort in the morning.

Would this be the stunning climax to the most ferocious campaign on American soil?

At The Cold Harbor Battlefield Park

Cold Harbor Battlefield Park is operated by the Hanover County Parks and Recreation Department. It shares a driveway with the Garthright House, operated by the National Park Service. Cold Harbor National Cemetery (in the background) is across the road. (CM)

Imagine witnessing not one but two horrific battles rage across your property. That would be the experience of the Garthrights, whose house stood in the way of attacking forces both in 1862 at Gaines Mill and then in 1864 at Cold Harbor. Parts of the house were believed to be over a century old by the time of the American Civil War. Members of the Garthright family took refuge in the basement during the Battle of Cold Harbor. Meanwhile, Miles Garthright, the owner of

the house, was serving in the Confederate cavalry and was actively engaged during the Cold Harbor battles. Imagine his wife, huddled in the basement as the Union assaults moved past the dwelling, hearing the trample of feet, the noise of battle, and knowing somewhere out there her husband was serving. Would he survive? Would the house survive?

After the battle, nearly 100 Union soldiers were buried in the front yard and around the Garthright house. These men were later disinterred and reburied in the Cold Harbor National Cemetery. (CM)

Modern houses now dot the landscape, but on June 1 and again on June 3, Union forces attacked here across an open plain. On June 1, Emory Upton launched his assault from the area you are now standing in. Two days later, it was John Gibbon's division who used this area as a staging point prior to their attack.

The nearby walking trail, about a mile long, will take you along the

Union lines. It was here that many soldiers clad in blue waited anxiously to be ordered toward the Confederate lines. What thoughts passed through their minds in those tense hours?

In this postwar photograph, Margaret Garthright, standing on the house steps, greets Union veterans visiting the battlefield. (NPS)

Similar to other massive assaults of the Civil War, the Federals undertook the task with a grim determination. The earthworks at Cold Harbor were the strongest that the Army of the Potomac had yet encountered, and every Union soldier tasked with making the charge knew what was in store as soon as they entered the no-man's-land.

Smith and Gibbon decided to replicate Upton's tactics by forming their men in a column

for the assault. Gibbon had participated in Hancock's assault on the Muleshoe Salient on May 12 and again on May 18 on another Confederate position. It was clear by the time the armies reached Cold Harbor that the value of Upton's tactics were impressing other Union officers.

Imagine the rate of fire the Union attackers faced: like walking into a steady hailstorm of lead. Incredibly, some of the regiments managed to withstand the enemy fire and reach to within yards of the enemy lines before being

The trail at Cold Harbor Battlefield Park runs along the Federal line. (DD/CM)

repulsed. Individual bravery, courage, and resolve were evident in abundance in the attacking Union soldiers. Likewise, though, the Confederates defending the trenches also gritted their teeth, unleashing volley after volley. Musket balls hit with a force akin to a modern baseball bat being swung hard and making contact with your chest.

"The field of heaviest losses," proclaims a roadside marker next to a set of Federal earthworks. Across the field in front of the earthworks just a few hundred yards sits the visitor center—and the Confederate position. After the assaults of June 1 and 3, 1864, the landscape between was littered with bodies. (DD/CM)

→ TO THE CONFEDERATE POSITION AT COLD HARBOR NATIONAL BATTLEFIELD (STOP 10)

Turn left out of the Garthright House parking lot and return to Tour Stop 8, the Cold Harbor Battlefield Visitor Center. Proceed past the Visitor Center along the park road and through the intervening ravine. Pull into the first parking lot on the right. Get out of your vehicle and stand next to the earthworks, looking out across the open field to your front.

"The Last Assault"
Part 1

CHAPTER NINE
JUNE 3, 1864

If there was any need for a reminder of what awaited men from both sides on the morning of June 3, that cue was found just below the surface. As Confederate infantry hurriedly improved their defenses, some of them discovered remains of either "friends or foes" that had fallen in this same area almost two years prior—to the day—at the battle of Gaines' Mill. By sunset, more remains would be added to the soil around Cold Harbor. The upcoming assault would live in the public memory that would forever shade opinions of Ulysses S. Grant's military career.

The men in William Smith's divisions had begun the spring campaign maneuvering up the James River until driven back at Drewry's Bluff below Richmond early in May. They had tested the Confederate lines at Cold Harbor two days earlier. Now, they were set to participate in the grand assault against Lee's lines.

For the attack, Smith decided to adopt Upton's tactic of forming his men in a solid column in the hopes of punching a hole through the enemy defenses. The divisions of Brig. Gens. William T. H. Brooks and John Martindale formed up in darkness of the early morning.

The Northern assaulting columns faced a Confederate line six miles in length. The Southerners' right flank faced due east, and as the line progressed

"No-man's land" between the lines at Cold Harbor National Battlefield (CM)

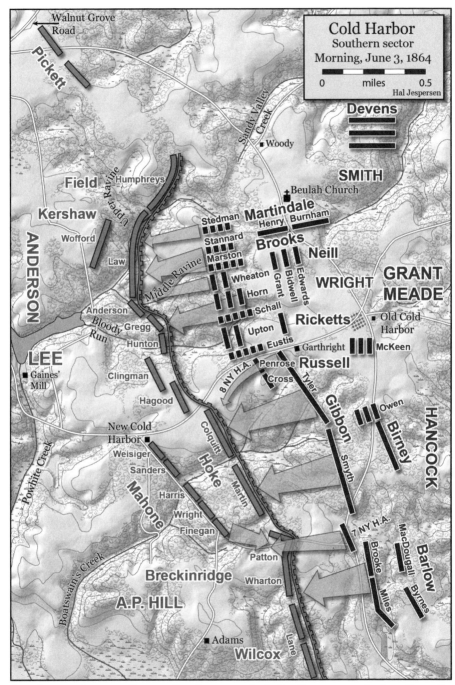

COLD HARBOR, SOUTHERN SECTOR—Grant's communiqué directing an assault along the entire Confederate line gets underway. Stepping off in the early morning, Hancock's II Corps attack gains some success. There, Union soldiers pierce the Confederate line. Intense hand-to-hand fighting, including a counterattack by Floridians and Confederate Marylanders, finally push back the Union breach. Smith's XVIII Corps also joins in the attack against the Confederate First Corps under Anderson. By early afternoon, the fighting has subsided.

Because only a portion of the battlefield is protected by the National Park Service, visitors can come to the misconception that the Federal attack on June 3 was much smaller than it really was. The area from the historical marker by the visitor center (left and below) to the northernmost loop in the park road represents only about one-quarter of the battle's southern sector. (DD/PG)

to the left, the formation fishhooked just enough that the left flank divisions—those of Maj. Gens. Harry Heth and Robert Rodes—faced south.

At Grant's appointed hour, a lone cannon shot signaled the advance, and Smith ordered his divisions forward. As the XVIII Corps advanced, wary Confederate pickets heard the tramp of thousands of approaching Northern soldiers and sounded the alarm. Picket shots rang out as comrades raced back to warn the main Confederate line.

A Connecticut soldier under Martindale remembered that his regiment "advanced through the woods toward the enemy's works which were in an open field . . . . Over this . . . space the regiment charged. . . . The men advanced with a cheer in excellent order, not a man flinching; but the fire of the enemy was very heavy."

The only bright spot was that some of the Rebel earthworks were near streams and ravines that could provide some protection for the advancing Federals but which would also severely disrupt their coordination. As the assaults progressed the ravines did not provide as much cover as hoped but provided enough distraction to break up cohesion.

Smith's Federals attacked across an expanse of a few hundred acres. The Confederate veterans waited for them, just as they had at the battle of Fredericksburg a year and a half prior. Firing from a protected position, they dropped the oncoming

Portions of the VI Corps attacked across this ground on June 3. (DD/PG)

Union soldiers in rows. The firing line was so crowded that—again, just as it was behind the stone wall at Marye's Heights in December of 1862— rifles were handed to the men in the front rank to fire and then passed back to be reloaded even as the men grabbed new rifles and kept firing.

Yet onward the Federals came. "The column moved . . . very soon encountering the fire of the enemy from their rifle-pits," wrote one Union officer:

The whole brigade sprang forward with loud cheers . . . quickly driving the enemy from their rifle-pits in front . . . the regiments passing over them and into the open space beyond. Here the fire of the rebels concealed in another line . . . was too murderous for any troops . . . to sustain. The ground was swept with canister and rifle-bullets until it was literally covered with the slain.

In an area of the line called the "Middle Ravine," the Union advance ran into the determined defenses of two Confederate divisions commanded by Brig. Gen. Joseph Kershaw and Maj. Gen. Charles Field. One Southern brigadier surveying that approach to the Confederate breastworks remembered the "writhing humanity." A veteran of many a battlefield, he wrote simply, "It was not war; it was murder." Another Southerner, with a nod toward the heroics of the Union XVIII Corps, wrote later that the action in the middle sector seemed "to be downright murder to kill men in the performance of an act so courageous."

On Smith's left, the VI Corps was getting under way, too. However, Horatio Wright recognized the futility in attacking such strong works, and he was not eager to send his men forward into the slaughter. Still, his men made the attempt.

"The rebels . . . held three lines of breastworks, all of great strength," a New Yorker recalled. "Amid the deafening volleys of musketry . . . our brave fellows pressed rapidly across the space between the hostile lines of works . . . but the works were too strong and the rebel forces too numerous. Their works could not be taken." Another wrote, "We advanced . . . under a heavy storm of lead . . . and halted under the crest of a small hill."

On June 1, this sector of the Confederate defense had been thinly held. Forty-eight hours later, that was no longer the case.

The Confederates under the command of Robert Hoke could hear the rising crescendo of small arms and artillery fire to their north and picking up to their south.

To the north of Hoke's divisions sat two First Corps brigades, Texans and Arkansans commanded by Brig. Gen. John Gregg and Georgians under the command of Brig. Gen. George "Tige" Anderson. They faced the stiffest test from the VI Corps when the brigade of Brig. Gen. Frank Wheaton came charging across the clearing in front of the lines.

But, the attack, according to one Texan, provided "the fairest of targets for Texas and Arkansas marksmanship," and was soundly defeated.

Wheaton's soldiers came to the same realization that gripped most of the VI Corps, including its commander: The enemy line could not be broken. Instinctively, they fell to the ground and began to dig in for protection.

Immediately adjacent to Wright was John Gibbon's II Corps division. Like Smith, Gibbon had formed his men to attack in column. "The country was rolling, in places intersected by ravines

. . . and my line was cut in two by a . . . swamp, which widened as we advanced toward the enemy," he wrote. "The troops pushed gallantly forward under a most terrific fire of cannon and musketry until close up to the enemy's works". Gibbon went on to say that his men "struggled against the heavy fire" and that his brigade's ranks were "much thinned" by the "bloody assault."

The II Corps attacked across the open expanse around the Garthright house (top). Some of that same ground remains open today (bottom). (LOC)(DD/PG)

An officer recalled that the 155th New York Infantry "advanced within 50 yards of the enemy's works, but owing to a deep ravine which intervened and the heavy fire from the enemy's breastworks, it was impossible for the regiment to gain the works. The regiment, however, held its ground for half an hour, returning the fire of the enemy vigorously, and only fell back when it was found useless to remain."

Here the II Corps faced Breckenridge's men, who had sealed the gap between Hoke's and Wilcox's divisions.

"Hell broke loose" along this front at approximately 4:30 a.m., and shortly thereafter a glimmer of hope, like the rising sun, broke over Hancock's veterans.

Almost miraculously, on Gibbon's left, elements of Francis Barlow's division were able to briefly penetrate the Confederate line. Commencing the assault, the 7th New York Heavy Artillery moved at the double-quick toward the Confederate lines. After the battle, an article in the *Richmond Sentinel* described the New Yorkers' advance: "They came gallantly forward, in spite of a severe fire and in spite of the loss of many of their men, who fell like autumn leaves, until the ground was almost blue and red with their uniforms and their blood."

Onward the regiment went, up a rise and, upon reaching the enemy works, finally opening with a scathing volley. Up and over and through the Rebels they went as both sides engaged in hand-to-hand combat. An onlooker wrote that the "grey backs were flying in all directions."

Joining the New Yorkers was the 5th New Hampshire from Col. Nelson Miles' brigade. "The rebels were driven from their [e]ntrenchments . . . leaving the guns and several prisoners in our possession," one New Hampshire officer later wrote. "After pursuing the retreating foe a short distance, the enemy's supports were encountered, and opened a galling cross-fire."

During the attack on June 3, Col. James McMahon fell at the head of the 164th New York Infantry. (LOC)

The New Yorkers retired under that galling fire, which came from the only reserve Maj. Gen. Breckenridge had on this portion of the line. Due to a mix-up in commands, a portion of the Confederate infantry had been recalled from the lines and sent to the rear, and only a reinforced skirmish line was manning the forward lines. Barlow's division attacked this very spot.

Breckenridge's reserve, 400 men belonging to the 2nd Maryland—the only Southern Maryland infantry unit—were resting behind the lines when the Union formations came out of the morning fog. One enterprising Maryland private shouted, "Let's charge 'm boys!" Another Marylander remembered what happened next: "We rush forward and charge the enemy, sending them back at the double-quick." Moving along to assist the Marylanders was a brigade of Floridians under Brig. Gen. Joseph Finegan.

A Confederate participant who helped push the Federals out of the captured works wrote afterwards

Once repulsed, the II Corps began to dig in again. (LOC)

that "the men were so excited . . . we rushed up . . . drove the enemy back and recovered the trenches."

Both sides settled down into exchanging fire, which one Union survivor of the II Corps assaults remembered being as hot as "the fury of hell."

Situated behind the lines, a surgeon in Wright's corps observed that it had "been the very worst day of the campaign . . . the woods full of dead, dying and wounded men. Literally heaps of dead men meet the eye on all sides! Stench like that of putrid carcasses, flavors your food, while the water is thick with all manner of impurities . . . on all sides booming cannon and rattling small arms tell us that the Angel of Death is hovering over us."

Grant's morning assault had failed miserably in front of Lee's impregnable lines. Any hope of Union success now rested to the north in the efforts of Ambrose Burnside and Gouverneur Warren.

Could these two men salvage the day and possibly end the war?

Near the park road pull-off on the Federals' side of no-man's land, a small row of concrete markers sticks out of the ground like teeth. While an old family burial ground was once located in the area, the markers do not indicate any gravesites, as some people believe. Rather, they simply mark the boundaries of a long-ago parking area. (CM)

➤ TO THE FEDERAL POSITION

Continue along the park road for 0.3 miles. The road parallels the Confederate position before cutting across the northernmost section of "no-man's land" and then looping back southward. Pull over at the parking area on the right.

As mentioned earlier in the text, much of the ground fought over at Bethesda Church has fallen victim to development, making it extremely difficult to view the battlefield. For the purposes of Chapter 10, please remain at the Federal position.

From the Confederate Position

Imagine that you are a Confederate soldier awakening in these earthworks on the morning of June 4. The first sound that greets you are the cries of the many Union wounded lying in the plain to your front. These men have spent a terrible day and night there since the attack the previous day.

A modern view from the Confederate perspective across no-man's land. (CM)

Limited shade and the early June sun are already taking a toll, and the wounded men are crying out for water, for help, and for loved ones. Tragically, salvation for many will not come.

From the Federal Position

As the morning of June 4 dawned, Union soldiers, awoke—if any had been able to sleep at all—both thankful and relieved. They were the survivors of yesterday's carnage. Even now, death still lingered. Stretching above the top of the earthworks could invite a sniper's bullet. Even

A modern view from the Federal perspective across no-man's land. (DD/PG)

around the campfires, shot and shell fired from Confederate artillery could come whistling at any time—drowning out, for a brief moment, the cries of suffering and anguish from comrades stranded in no-man's land.

"The Last Assault"
Part II

CHAPTER TEN
JUNE 3, 1864

Remembering the events of June 3 years later, an Alabama surgeon recalled a simple observation he'd made of the Union general in chief. Grant was a "much more stubborn Gen. than we have ever fought before."

Before the day was out, many Union soldiers would agree with the Alabaman's post-battle assessment.

As Hancock, Wright, and Smith slammed against the Confederate works around Cold Harbor, Burnside and Warren were girding to assault Early's lines north of Bethesda Church. Perhaps because of Early's swift attack the day before, the two corps commanders were slow in getting under way. They did not begin their movement until well after Grant's designated time.

At approximately 6:30 a.m., the ball commenced when Federals on the left advanced toward Rebels ensconced along Shady Grove Road. Facing the oncoming V Corps were the Second Corps divisions of Maj. Gen. John Gordon and Maj. Gen. Robert Rodes. The approaches to the Confederate lines were through a cleared field. The Confederates had converted former Union entrenchments into more formidable defenses that looked out across a cleared field toward the advancing blue waves. "We did not wait long until the lines of blue coats were seen advancing in splendid order," one Confederate remembered.

A New Englander serving with Sweitzer wrote that the line's "center came under as galling a

Earthworks still criss-cross the landscape near the battlefield visitor center, marking the Confederate position. (CM)

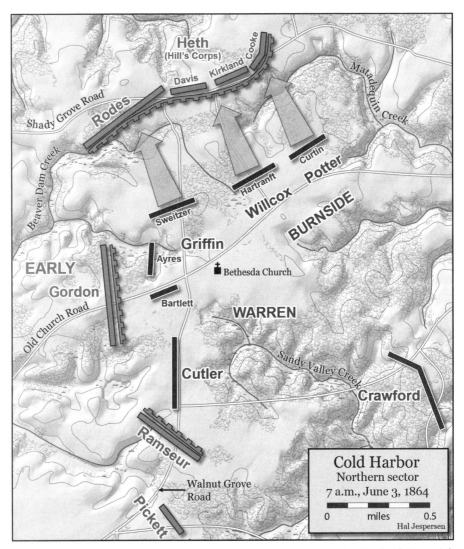

COLD HARBOR, NORTHERN SECTOR—Ambrose Burnside's IX Corps attacks the Confederate left flank, held by Jubal Early's Second Corps. As the IX Corps overruns the Confederate picket line entrenchments, Burnside mistakenly believes he has overrun the main Confederate line. A lengthy pause ensues, which allows for the Confederates to strengthen. Although Burnside initially lays plans to continue the assault in the early afternoon, the attack is suspended. Today, this ground is off preserved property.

musketry fire that I ever experienced on a skirmish. The men availed themselves of fences, trees and old outhouses . . . for protection." Sweitzer's men reached to within from "100 to 200 yards of the enemy's works" but could go no farther.

On Sweitzer's right, the IX Corps brigades of Brig. Gens. John Curtin and John Hartranft joined

in the attack. "The lines advanced in elegant style," Hartranft recalled, "driving the enemy from the pits and occupied the same, which were within 200 yards of the enemy's main line . . . . His infantry, in his lines stretching off to my left, enfiladed my line . . . . The troops made temporary cover by using their bayonets, tin cups, plates."

Maj. Gen. Ambrose Burnside (seated, center) with his staff (LOC)

One Rhode Island soldier remembered that the Confederates were

> *[e]ntrenched in two lines . . . their first line on the edge of a deep swamp that was covered by a thicket of brush and sprouts, and the second on a ridge beyond. We crossed our [e]ntrenchments . . . charged . . . carried their first line and took position within 60 yards of their second, returned their galling fire, and soon after commenced constructing cover, which was at first slow work . . . like the swelling and ebbing of the voice of the winds, the noise of battle now rose to a hurricane and now sank to a whisper.*

Like their comrades, though, the men in Sweitzer's, Curtin's, and Hartranft's brigades ground to a halt before the Confederate works.

One Federal "would never forget the storm of bullets, grape, and canister" that belched from the Confederate lines.

Although some of Burnside's men were able to carry the field works thrown up by the Confederate skirmish line, they barely tested the main line held by the still-formidable Second Corps divisions. "Our boys had good works to fight behind," wrote one Georgian of the assaults. "I know they [comrades] poured it to them right."

The thousands of corpses littering "no-man's land" could attest to the fact. The Yankees caught in that forsaken area, who were digging and sheltering "ourselves as best we could," might have used stronger language in their agreement.

*   *   *

Throughout the morning, dispatches streamed into Meade's headquarters. Barlow's temporary breakthrough had shown some promise. As the hours wore on, though, it became clear that little headway could be made by the Union divisions. Unrelenting, Meade continued to send directives to his corps commanders to push the lines forward. Grant encouraged his conduct, instructing that "the moment it becomes certain that an assault cannot succeed, suspend the offensive, but when one does succeed push it vigorously."

Finally, early in the afternoon, the Federal high command decided to cease offensive operations.

The killing fields of Cold Harbor fell mostly silent.

Death's harvest would claim a few more lives that evening. The attacks by the II Corps, particularly Barlow's division, had halted dangerously close to the Rebel lines. Apparently, it was too close for comfort for Colonel Finegan's Floridians.

A contingent of the 2nd Florida Infantry sallied forth. With the customary "Rebel Yell," they jumped over the earthworks and made the dash. As one eyewitness remembered, "Their one and only consolation was consciousness of duty performed." That duty ended less than a hundred yards from their own lines. All of the Floridians who made the charge were killed.

Shortly thereafter, some Tar Heels tried to push back some of Gibbon's men who had ended up too close to their works. Who issued the orders for the attack still remains a mystery. Their fate, like their brethren from the Sunshine State, was the same. Union troops "poured in heavy volleys of musketry," and the Confederates never had a chance. Fortunately, not all of the North Carolinians shared the fate of Finegan's men.

By late evening, the attacks from both sides were finally over.

*   *   *

"I have always regretted the last assault at Cold Harbor was made," Grant wrote in his memoirs after the war. "At Cold Harbor, no advantage whatever was gained to compensate for the heavy loss we sustained. Indeed the advantages . . . were on the Confederate side."

Grant's counterpart in command, Robert E. Lee, saw it in the same light. "Our loss today has been small and our success, under the blessing of God, all that we could expect," he reported to the Confederate Secretary of War. He bedded down on the night of June 3 behind a near-impregnable Confederate defensive network.

Casualties attributed for the assault typically rest around 7,000, but this figure may be closer to the losses suffered on both June 1 and June 3. Somewhere around 4,000 men fell on June 3 alone. This number is significantly less than the 8,000 Union soldiers who fell in front of Marye's Heights at Fredericksburg or the 6,000-plus Confederate soldiers lost in Pickett's Charge at Gettysburg.

Charles Dana, the U.S. Assistant Secretary of War who had accompanied Grant and his staff throughout the campaign, succinctly captured the night of June 3 when the guns fell silent. "Nothing can give a greater idea of deathless tenacity of purpose," he wrote, "than the picture . . . after a bloody and nearly continuous struggle for thirty days [by the men in both armies] . . . lying down to sleep, with their heads almost on each other's throats!"

⟶ **TO COLD HARBOR NATIONAL CEMETERY (STOP 11)**

Continue along the Park Road until it ends at Rt. 156. Turn left and to your immediate left front, you will see the entrance and pull off for the Cold Harbor National Cemetery.

Leaving the park, .25 miles past the pull-off at the Federal side of no-man's land, visitors pass the monument for the 2nd Connecticut Heavy Artillery—"Connecticut Remembers Her Fallen Sons." (DD/PG)

E 130

BATTLE OF COLD HARBOR: FLAG OF TRUCE

On 5 June 1864, two hot days after Gen. Robert E. Lee's bloody repulse of Gen. Ulysses S. Grant's frontal assault, Federal Lt. Col. Theodore Lyman met Confederate Maj. Thomas J. Wooten nearby on Cold Harbor Road to initiate written communication on the plight of the Union wounded between the lines. Confederate Gen. A. P. Hill's trenches stood 800 yards west, and skirmishers' rifle pits survive only 200 yards away. Because Lee and Grant disagreed on terms, two more days elapsed before they observed a two-hour flag of truce. Only a few wounded Federals were found alive. The remainder had either died, crawled to safety, or been retrieved under cover of darkness.

DEPARTMENT OF HISTORIC RESOURCES, 2005

Flag of Truce

CHAPTER ELEVEN

JUNE 4-5, 1864

Writing on June 4, surgeon Daniel Holt observed that it was "quite a quiet day" compared to "three of such fearful slaughter." Union and Confederate soldiers understandably remained on edge, though. "Both sides were . . . sensitive," one of Meade's staff officers recalled. "The slightest movement would provoke a volley, and any unusual stir would open a battery . . . . All the day there was sharpshooting and cannonading along our front."

"The boys are amusing themselves by firing through loop holes at every rebel that shows his head," a Union officer said. It was grim amusement, indeed, in the aftermath of what had occurred over the previous few days.

On the Confederate side, the army spent the night reshaping lines and reorganizing units. Usually troops would grumble at these tasks when the sun fell, but Southern morale ran high that night— despite all the hard marching, the unpredictable rations, the cries of the wounded being heard from no-man's-land, and the high probability that the men would become casualties themselves. No matter what lay in the future, said one Confederate, "all felt such unbounded confidence" in Marse Robert.

"My men were moving at route step," said a member of Heth's division, which had served with Early's Second during the battle but which had been ordered out of line during the nighttime lull to

As Grant and Lee dickered over how to save them, hundreds of men died in the Virginia heat. (DD)

Days of fighting left the landscape stripped bare, with thousands of bodies—living and dead—strewn between the lines. (LOC)

rendezvous with the rest of the Third Corps. "[A]nd, as was usual on a march, were laughing, talking, singing or whistling." When the men approached Lee's headquarters, though, a murmur went down the lines. "'Hush, boys, don't make a noise,'" the officer recalled. "'There is Marse Robert asleep under that tree.' Instantly there was perfect silence."

These brief moments of respectful silence, on both sides, were squashed by the sounds coming from no-man's-land—curses, cries, moans, whimpers. Accompanying the soundtrack of agony were the sudden cracks of snipers' rifles and the whizzing of single bullets. All too often, there was the sick sound of a bullet striking flesh or bone.

The killing did not stop, as "thousands of men [were] cramped in a narrow trench, unable to get out, or get up," one soldier said. "A man's life often exacted as the price of a cup of water from the spring."

"Never before had our army been in a position where there was such constant danger," one member of the 77th New York remembered:

Men in the front line dared not leave the cover of the breastworks . . . . High breastworks were thrown up at all angles with the main line and deep trenches were dug, in which the men might pass to and from the front without being observed . . . . The army lay upon the burning sands of that arid plain, the greater part of the line without the friendly shelter of the tree.

The chasm between enlisted man and officer was typically vast and deep, but Cold Harbor bridged that gulf. Like the soldier from the Empire State, Brig. Gen. John Gibbon wrote:

The weather was intensely hot and notwithstanding

As time wore on, the armies harassed each other with sniping and artillery fire. (B&L)

the rain of the day before, the fine sandy soil soon turned to dust. On some parts of the line . . . no water was to be had . . . until darkness enabled the men to crawl back and supply themselves and their comrades from a stream near by, to connect with which a trench was dug . . . and by this means communication was established to the rear. In the meantime our killed and wounded lay out in the space between the two lines.

That night, more rain came, yet it was little comfort to the men on either side, especially to those Union soldiers lying in front of the Confederate works. Thousands of wounded Federals lay stranded where they had fallen during the June 3 assault.

After receiving an inquiry from Hancock, Meade asked Grant if anything could be done about retrieving the wounded. Grant in turn penned a note to Lee. "It is reported to me that there are wounded men . . . lying . . . between the lines," he wrote. "I would propose . . . when no battle is raging . . . men bearing litters to pick up their dead and wounded."

Lee acknowledged Grant's letter but strictly followed the dictates of the rules of war. His response put the metaphorical ball back in Grant's court. "I propose, therefore, instead, that when either party desires to remove their dead and wounded, a flag of truce be sent, as is customary," Lee wrote.

Grant, not wanting to admit to a flag of truce—in itself an admission of defeat—responded the next day. Trying to side-step the prickly admission of loss, Grant wrote: "I will send immediately, as

Both sides fortified so much that one Federal soldier said he and his comrades lived like gophers. (LOC)

you propose, to collect the dead and wounded between the lines . . . and will instruct that you be allowed to do the same."

However, the Confederate commander insisted that his counterpart follow the proper military protocol. Lee's response to Grant's communiqué emphasized his "regret . . . that I did not make myself understood in my communication of yesterday." He "could not consent to the burial of the dead and the removal of the wounded . . . in the way you propose, but that when either party desire such permission it shall be asked by flag of truce in the usual way."

Even in negotiating a brief truce, these warriors were unrelenting. The two would exchange letters until June 7, when Grant finally consented and sent the flag of truce. The Federals were allowed to finally bring in some their comrades—those who were still living, anyway. Scores had died, however, during the war of words between the two generals.

In the meantime, the general in chief had been thinking and planning. Despite the carnage of Cold Harbor, "General Grant means to hold on," a Rhode Island officer predicted, "and I know that he will win in the end."

On display at the Cold Harbor Visitor Center: a canteen reshaped for use as a shovel for digging. (CM)

At Cold Harbor National Cemetery

If there was ever a moment that Lee gained the upper hand on Grant, it was during the truce negotiations following the battle. For Grant to formally request a white flag across the lines to collect his wounded was, within the context of nineteenth century warfare, a declaration of defeat. This was a defeat that Grant could ill afford. 1864 was a Presidential election year. The election itself would be a referendum on Abraham Lincoln's administration and its ability to emerge from the war victorious. Any flag of truce sent forth by Grant would have serious consequences, and Lee knew it. It was quite possibly why he was so stringent on observing the proper protocols in his correspondence with Grant.

The Cold Harbor National Cemetery sits across the street from the Hanover County park. (DD/PG)

Meanwhile, thousands of Union soldiers perished in the June sun while the two commanders traded letters and haggled over military decorum. Although Grant viewed it as a matter of honor and principle, the men in the lines heard the nerve-wracking, gut-wrenching cries for "water" or "mercy" as comrades, friends, and relatives, laid in no-man's land. It was a grim example of the harshness of war.

Two-thousand two-hundred and ten individuals are interred at the Cold Harbor National Cemetery. (PG)

The Cold Harbor National Cemetery was founded in 1866. The lodge and enclosing brick wall were constructed five years later. The total cost in acquiring the acreage necessary by the U.S. Government was $500. There is one Medal of Honor recipient buried in the cemetery, Sergeant Major Augustus Barry. Barry was a soldier in the 16th U.S. Infantry who received the medal for "gallantry in various actions" during the Civil War. Barry also served as one of the first Superintendents of the cemetery. Today, the cemetery is administered by the Hampton National Cemetery and is currently closed for new internments.

As you walk inside, to your immediate left stands a monument honoring soldiers from Pennsylvania. To your immediate left front is a monument to the 8th New York Heavy Artillery. Commanded by Col. Peter Porter, the regiment formed up for the June 3 assault in what is now the Cold Harbor Park. During the attack, Porter was killed at the head of the regiment and fell only yards away from the Confederate entrenchments. The regiment would be pinned down near the Confederate lines and

would not be able to withdraw until nightfall. Under the cover of dark, Sgt. LeRoy Williams managed to retrieve Porter's body, earning him the Medal of Honor.

Toward the rear of the cemetery is a mass grave of 898 soldiers who were killed during the 1862 and 1864 battles around Richmond.

Top left: The Pennsylvania monument (PG)

Top right: The 8th New York Heavey Artillery monument (PG)

Below: Tomb of the Unknown Soldiers (PG)

→ **TO THE JAMES RIVER (OPTIONAL)**

Turn left onto Cold Harbor Road (Rt. 156). In half a mile, turn right to stay on Rt. 156. In 2.7 miles turn left onto Market Road (Rt. 630). In 5.8 miles, turn right onto Market Highway (Rt. 249). Remain on Market Highway as it turns into Rt. 33. In 4 miles, turn left onto Pocahontas Trail (Rt.60 E). Follow Rt. 60 for 1.3 miles and turn right onto Roxbury Road (Rt. 609, Rt. 106 South). In 3.7 miles turn left to stay on Rt. 609. In 3 miles, veer left onto Lott Cary Road (Rt. 602). In 4.5 miles, turn right on Adkins Road (Rt. 618). Ahead, may a left onto John Tyler Memorial Highway (Rt. 5). Make the first left onto Wilcox Wharf Road. Follow Wilcox Wharf Road to the end and pull into the parking lot. A Virginia Civil War Trails Sign is at the end of the parking lot.

South to the James

CHAPTER TWELVE

JUNE 5, 1864

A simple fact was clear to Grant on the morning of June 5: any further efforts at Cold Harbor were fruitless.

The campaign had been characterized by an evolution in defensive warfare and the efforts of such enterprising officers as Emory Upton to counter these tactics. Similar to Upton's Charge on May 10 and Winfield Scott Hancock's assault on the Muleshoe on May 12, the June 3 attack of the 7th New York Heavy Artillery had become the metaphor for Union offensive operations: grand assaults against fortified positions that were initially successful but, for one reason or another, were never followed through to a victorious conclusion by the Federal high command.

At Cold Harbor, Grant had been stymied by these factors—massive field fortifications and the inability to exploit hard-won advantages—as much as by Lee's army, depriving him of what he yearned for the most: to extinguish, like a candle, the Army of Northern Virginia.

While he was dickering with Lee about the temporary ceasefire, Grant was also writing to Washington. "My idea from the start has been to beat Lee's army if possible, north of Richmond," he explained. "I now find after over thirty days of trial, the enemy deems of this first importance to run no new risk with the armies they now have. They

Wilcox's Landing along the James River (DD)

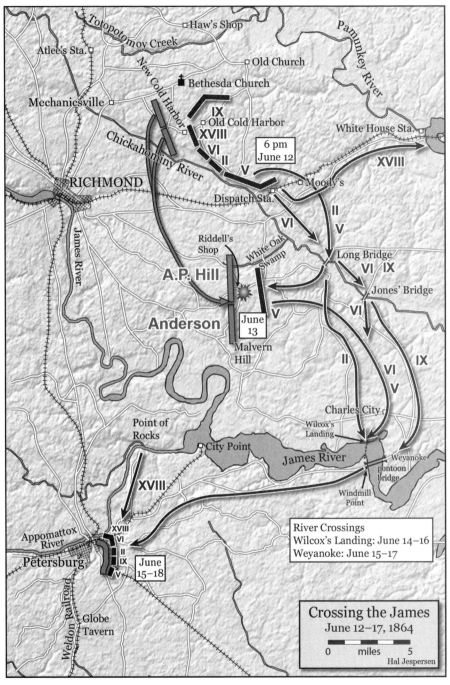

CROSSING THE JAMES—After Lee thwarted Grant at Cold Harbor, the Union general-in-chief decided to cross the James River, shifting his focus to the capture of Petersburg—a change in philosophy from the Overland Campaign in which his mission was to destroy Lee's forces. Lee worried that if the Confederates could not destroy Grant north of the James River, then it was just "a mere question of time" before Confederate defeat. He was right, but the outcome would be nine months in the making.

"AS HE SAT AT HIS DESK WRITING DISPATCHES AND CHEWING ON A CIGAR, GRANT MAY VERY WELL HAVE NOTICED A MAP OF VIRGINIA. TRACING HIS INDEX FINGER FROM HIS CURRENT POSITION TO THE SOUTHWEST BROUGHT HIS EYES TO THE CITY OF PETERSBURG . . . ." (LOC)

act purely on the defensive behind breastworks . . . without a greater sacrifice of human life than I am willing to make all cannot be accomplished that I had designed."

As he sat at his desk writing dispatches and chewing on a cigar, Grant may very well have noticed a map of Virginia. Tracing his index finger from his current position to the southwest brought his eyes to the city of Petersburg, Virginia.

That spring, as Grant engaged in the great chess match with Lee, his top subordinate, Maj. Gen. William Tecumseh Sherman, was leading Union armies through Georgia toward Atlanta. It was the logistical center of the Deep South. Four railroads converged in the vicinity of the city. Petersburg was an even bigger hub, where five lines joined together. Of those five, only one ran north to Richmond. Petersburg was just as large a prize as Atlanta.

Reverting to the strategy now being executed by Sherman, Grant decided to shift his focus from Lee to Lee's logistics. If Grant could carry Petersburg, Richmond and Lee's army would be at his mercy.

The Overland Campaign took a terrible toll on the leadership of the Army of Northern Virginia—from corps commanders like Maj. Gen. Jeb Stuart, killed at Yellow Tavern (above), down through brigade commanders like Brig. Gen. George "Maryland" Steuart (below), captured at Spotsylvania. (DD/PG) (LOC)

A week later, the Army of the Potomac began withdrawing from its lines at Cold Harbor, bound for the James River and, beyond it, Petersburg. When the armies marched away from the ravaged crossroads of Cold Harbor, they left behind the mangled corpses and broken bodies of 15,500. The Overland Campaign's final harvest was over.

Lee failed to destroy the Federal army before it reached the James River, which it did on June 14, almost completely unmolested. Thanks to a massive engineering effort, the army slipped south of the river overnight. Thus, Lee's onetime prophecy was coming true: "We must destroy this Army of Grant's before he gets to the James River," the Gray Fox had said to his Bad Old Man that spring. "If he gets there it will become a siege and then it will be a mere question of time."

It must have been frustrating for Lee, who had thwarted Grant's every move for a month and a half yet still found himself backed against the gates of Richmond.

At least the morale of his army—for the majority—was still ticking on the positive side. The army was "in fine spirits," wrote Lee's diligent staff officer, Col. Walter Taylor. One hopeful Confederate even wrote home to say that he had "heard General Lee tell General Hoke that the campaign would be over in a month . . . . I expect the great battle will come off before this letter reaches you."

Losses, though, from the officer corps down through the ranks highlighted the fact that Grant's bulldog tenacity was slowly achieving its objective. Nearly half of Lee's army—approximately 30,000 to 35,000 of the 66,000 soldiers that had buoyantly jaunted down the roads on May 5—had been killed, wounded, or captured.

Of the three infantry corps commanders who started the campaign, Lt. Gen. James Longstreet had been severely wounded at the Wilderness; Lt. Gen. Richard Ewell had gone on sick leave and never been reinstated after North Anna; and Lt. Gen. A. P. Hill had been incapacitated for large portions of the campaign with varying illnesses.

Moving one rung down on the ladder, a whole division was practically wiped out at Spotsylvania Court House when Maj. Gen. Edward "Alleghany" Johnson's division collapsed at the Mule Shoe Salient. The number of killed, wounded, and captured reached roughly 4,000 men, including Johnson and Brig. Gen. George H. Steuart, and some of the most renowned regiments in the army, including the Stonewall Brigade and the Louisiana Tigers.

Attrition amongst infantry brigade officers was evident, too. Two brigadier generals were killed at the Wilderness and a third would die of wounds. Five more were wounded and knocked out of action for varying lengths of time. At Spotsylvania, three more officers fell during the fighting, three were mortally wounded, nine were injured, and two were captured. At Cold Harbor, one more brigade commander fell, another was mortally wounded, and four suffered injuries. Even taking into account Gen. John Breckenridge's reinforcements from the Shenandoah Valley, Maj. Gen. Robert Hoke's division from Petersburg, and the First Corps division of Maj. Gen. George Pickett, Lee had at most 41 brigades of infantry. Of them, 30 brigade officers were killed, captured, or wounded during the month-long campaign.

Insignia of the Federal II Corps. The Corps started the campaign as Grant's most dependable hammer—but by Cold Harbor, it had bled out dramatically. (DD/PG)

The Confederate cavalry corps was hit just as hard, with the most pressing loss being its commander, Maj. Gen. J. E. B. Stuart, who was mortally wounded at Yellow Tavern on May 11.

For the North, officer attrition was not as high, but still spoke volumes to the charnel house that was the Overland Campaign. The Army of the Potomac boasted three corps plus the addition of Burnside's IX Corps. John Sedgewick, in charge of the VI Corps, was killed on May 9 at Spotsylvania.

The Union forces boasted 13 divisions on May 5; by the time these units marched away from Cold Harbor, two division commanders had been mortally wounded or killed, two were wounded, and still another was relieved.

Brigade commanders in the Army of the

Grant's army reached the James River on June 14; by June 17, it was entirely across and on the move toward the vital Confederate supply junction of Petersburg. (LOC)

Potomac also suffered accordingly: four were mortally wounded or killed, nine were wounded, three were captured, five were disabled in some capacity, and two were relieved because of drunkenness. Thus, out of the 40 brigades in the four corps, 23 commanders became casualties of the campaign. Even the XVIII Corps suffered a mortally wounded brigade commander when the corps joined the Army of the Potomac during the Cold Harbor campaign.

For the Union cavalry, the command structure stayed consistent throughout with the exception of one division commander who relinquished command because of sickness.

In short, Lee and his legions had endured an incredible pounding at the hands of Grant. One Confederate foot soldier summed up the attrition—not just in the officer corps or in the Confederate army, but in general—with a simple question: "How many more good men must pour out their blood?"

That answer lay on the other side of the James River and nine more months of bloodshed.

Although neither side could have known it, the longest siege in American history was about to begin.

Opposite: Following the end
of the war, burial parties
returned to the battlefields to
inter the dead. John Reekie,
who worked for Matthew
Brady, returned to Cold Harbor
to document the grim work,
and he captured this somber
image. It has become one of
the most enduring images
of the war. Another Brady
associate, Alexander Gardner,
printed the photograph in
*Gardner's Photographic
Sketch Book of the War*. (LOC)

A flagpole stands at the center of Cold Harbor National Cemetery. (PG)

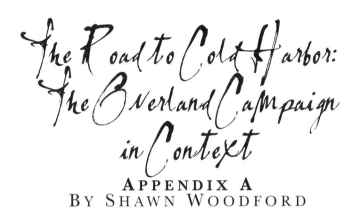

APPENDIX A
BY SHAWN WOODFORD

The battle of Cold Harbor was both the culmination of and transition point in Ulysses S. Grant's effort to engage and defeat Confederate forces under Robert E. Lee in open battle. The month-long series of battles known as the Overland Campaign constituted the main effort of Grant's overall strategic plan to defeat the last remaining Confederate armies in Virginia and Georgia.

Political considerations defined the campaign. By 1864, both presidents—Abraham Lincoln and Jefferson Davis—had clearly articulated their war aims. Lincoln eloquently reiterated in his November 1863 Gettysburg Address that the fundamental purpose of the struggle for the North was to restore the Union and preserve American democracy. His Emancipation Proclamation of 1862 made the destruction of slavery a militarily necessary precondition for reunion.

For Davis, the war had one goal: Southern independence. He never deviated from the view he expressed in 1861: "We have entered upon the career of independence, and it must be inflexibly pursued . . . . A reunification with the states from which we have separated is neither practical nor desirable." As historian William C. Davis observed, "Lincoln would negotiate anything but disunion; Davis would negotiate only on the basis of [southern] independence." Each man understood that no peace was possible short of unconditional victory by one side or the other. Lincoln summed it up clearly in his second inaugural address: "[Jefferson Davis] cannot voluntarily reaccept the Union; we cannot voluntarily yield it. Between him and us the issue is distinct, simple, and inflexible. It is an issue that can only be tried by war, and decided by victory."

* * *

Lincoln governed a divided polity and faced a referendum on his leadership

President Lincoln faced a deeply divided electorate. A lack of battlefield victories, especially in the East, eroded public support for the war. (LOC)

in the forthcoming November 1864 presidential election. To maintain public support for the war and his presidency, Lincoln needed to demonstrate battlefield success. To that end, he summoned Ulysses S. Grant, the most successful Union commander to date, to become general in chief of the army.

Grant's ascent to supreme command came only after a political dance with Lincoln. Though the president had long supported Grant, Lincoln remained wary of empowering a potential political rival. Grant's political patron, Illinois Republican Congressman Elihu B. Washburne, conveyed Grant's requirements to accept higher military responsibility: promotion to lieutenant general and overall command of Union armies. Washburne introduced legislation to revive the defunct top rank, but Lincoln supported it only after Grant made explicit his lack of political ambitions. Lincoln promoted Grant and named him general in chief on March 9.

Lincoln had exercised his prerogative as commander-in-chief over Union strategy and military operations, mostly in the Eastern Theater, with increasing assertiveness since early 1862. Lincoln's views on the conduct of the war in the East were conveyed to Grant in early 1864, before Grant became general-in-chief. Grant had been discussing strategic options in the western theater with then-general-in-chief, Maj. Gen. Henry Halleck since late 1863. In January 1864, Halleck solicited Grant's views on strategy in the east.

Grant proposed a strategic raid against Confederate railroads and supply areas in southern Virginia and North Carolina. He believed this would force Lee to abandon Richmond and Virginia. Like Maj. Gen. George G. Meade, commander of the Army of the Potomac, Grant believed the most logical course of action was to move against the Confederate capital and main base for Lee's Army of Northern Virginia along the line of the James River.

Grant thought this approach promised more decisive results than moving directly against Lee's forces.

Halleck's reply on February 17, three weeks before Grant became general-in-chief, contained a detailed critique of Grant's suggestion and made clear that Lincoln would not approve any operations that risked the safety of Washington, D.C. or did not directly target Lee's army. In his memoirs, Grant would recall that upon his initial meeting with Lincoln on his arrival in Washington, D.C. in March, the president stated that had not intended to interfere in military affairs, but had been forced to by the "procrastination on the part of commanders, and pressure from the people at the North and Congress." Lincoln then told Grant he did not want to know what plan of campaign the general had in mind. However, Grant's memoirs did not mention his recent correspondence with Halleck or the fact that Grant was already well aware of Lincoln's strategic preferences before their meeting.

Confederate President Davis suffered from an acute case of "States' Rights"—an inability to get Southern states to contribute equally and in coordinated fashion to the war effort. (LOC)

Politically astute enough to understand that challenging Lincoln over this would be unwise, Grant instead developed a campaign plan that reconciled the president's intent with his own belief in the necessity to directly threaten Richmond. The basic concept of Grant's overall plan was simultaneous offensives by Union forces in the western and eastern theaters to prevent the Confederacy from shifting its forces in response.

Union armies in the east would also carry out a series of simultaneous attacks. While the Army of the Potomac advanced south, seeking to bring Lee to battle in the open, a newly constituted Army of the James under Maj. Gen. Benjamin Butler would land along the James River and move on Richmond from the south. Grant believed that seizing the Confederate army's base of operations and engaging it between two powerful Union armies could decisively damage it and potentially force its capitulation. In a supporting raid into the Shenandoah Valley, Maj. Gen. Franz Sigel intended to break up the Virginia and Tennessee railroad and prevent local forces there from reinforcing Lee. Grant tried to replace Butler and Sigel—who owed their positions to political patronage—with more trusted officers, but Lincoln would not permit it.

*   *   *

As Union fortunes had brightened, the outlook for President Jefferson Davis and the Confederate States of America had declined. Like Lincoln, Davis presided over a divided constituency. Just as victories had buoyed Lincoln's political support, defeats nearly cost Davis his supporting majority in the autumn congressional elections, forcing his administration into political coalitions. Since the Confederacy lacked political parties, the opposition was less unified, but no less pointed. Deep disagreements existed over Davis's wartime policies on conscription, *habeas corpus*, impressment of produce and livestock to feed the armies, and taxation, among others. Davis's bitter critics in the Confederate Congress constantly challenged the president's management of the war. They raked him publicly over the defeats at Vicksburg and Chattanooga and for his choice of field commanders. Davis's relationships with key governors, including Zebulon Vance of North Carolina, were similarly contentious.

This political turmoil directly affected the Confederate war effort. Mismanagement of government finances and war economics drove prices for commodities up and inflated the currency. Difficulty finding supplies and adequate manpower to sustain the armies imposed additional hardships on the population, which provoked passive political resistance in the form of soldier absenteeism and desertion. The difficulties in supplying the Army of Northern Virginia along the Rapidan River led Lee to disperse it throughout Virginia and North Carolina by the end of 1863.

Unlike Lincoln, Davis did not entrust military supreme command to one of his generals, although he had a commander he fully trusted in Lee. A West Point graduate and former Secretary of War, Davis believed in his own abilities. Davis did not heed Lee's recommendation in early 1864 that the Army of Northern Virginia be reassembled and reinforced to launch a preemptive offensive against Grant's forces concentrating in Virginia. Though Lee approved of using his troops in minor operations elsewhere, by the end of March he called upon Davis to return them to Virginia. It would not be until the first week of April that detached elements of Lee's army in east Tennessee began moving back toward Virginia.

Lee had accurately divined Grant's strategic intentions by mid-April, and he urgently called on Davis again to reunite his army. Davis instead allowed an attack on the Federal enclave at Plymouth, North Carolina, to continue until April 20. Though the attack was successful and perhaps cultivated some favor for Davis with state politicians, it had no strategic impact. By the time Lee's detachments were finally released by local departmental commanders, the shaky Confederate railroads could not accommodate them all, and a bottleneck developed in Richmond, delaying their transport.

When the Army of the Potomac began its anticipated offensive on May 4, the Army of Northern Virginia remained incomplete—none of the reinforcing brigades from South Carolina, Georgia, or Florida had arrived. Recent detailed studies of Confederate manpower suggest that despite the challenges it faced, the Army of Northern Virginia had been rebuilt following the bloodletting at Gettysburg. If Davis had permitted all of the detached elements to be reunited in time, Lee's army would have been nearly the same size as it had been in June 1863. Further, it could have been augmented sooner by the veteran brigades that finally did arrive in the weeks following. Rather than a 1:2 manpower disadvantage, Lee could have enjoyed a much more reasonable disparity and enough extra troops to allow him more options for offensive action.

*   *   *

The Army of the Potomac crossed Germanna Ford beginning on May 4—and Grant's master plan began to unravel almost at once. (CM)

Grant's offensive plan miscarried from the beginning. The Army of the Potomac crossed the Rappahannock River on May 4-5 and turned Lee's right flank. Rather than marching completely through the densely forested Wilderness before engaging the Confederates, as Grant and Meade had hoped, the Federals halted and turned to face the approaching enemy, allowing Lee to fight them to a draw on terrain favorable to the Confederates, in a two-day battle. Butler's Army of James landed on banks of the James River on May 5, but his slow and tentative advance on Richmond was easily thwarted by a much smaller force under Gen. Pierre G. T. Beauregard. Sigel's advance into the Shenandoah was stopped by troops led by Maj. Gen. John C. Breckenridge at the battle of New Market on May 15. Despite Grant's best efforts, the Army of the Potomac was left to face off with the Army of Northern Virginia alone.

With the collapse of his operational concept, Grant nonetheless remained resolved to carry out Lincoln's intent. After narrowly failing to outflank

Lee in a race to take a key road junction near Spotsylvania Court House on May 7-8, Grant subjected the Confederates to a series of frontal assaults during the next week. Grant probed for another opening to attack, but Lee provided none, so Grant again turned Lee's right and moved south until the Army of Northern Virginia again blocked the Federals at the North Anna River. There again Grant moved around Lee's right, a move that brought the armies together at Cold Harbor on the outskirts of Richmond.

Following the repulse at Cold Harbor, Grant abandoned the attempt to defeat Lee directly and reverted to the strategy he had advocated at the beginning of the year. Although he notified Lincoln of his intentions beforehand, Grant did not seek his permission before shifting the Army of the Potomac to the James River and attempting to cut Richmond's supplies and communication by taking Petersburg. When that gambit failed, Grant pinned Lee's forces in the Petersburg and Richmond fortifications and sought to damage them with limited offensive operations designed to gradually cut their rail and canal lifelines. Grant had reached the coveted James River position and locked Lee into a state of semi-siege, but Richmond remained in Confederate hands. Consequently, by mid-June 1864, the main effort of Union strategic operations shifted out of necessity to Maj. Gen. William T. Sherman's campaign to defeat the Confederate Army of Tennessee in Georgia. Lee was thereafter able to wrest a measure of initiative back from Grant by sending a force into the Shenandoah Valley that succeeded in delaying a concentration of overwhelming numbers against Richmond and Petersburg until early 1865.

Grant was labelled a butcher for the massive casualties the Union suffered in the Overland Campaign, but in truth, his campaign plan had been defined by Lincoln, who overruled proposed alternatives. As Grant, Meade, and many other senior Union officers suspected, destroying Lee's army in combat was probably beyond the Union's

A *Harper's Weekly* artist caught the Federal artillery in action at Cold Harbor. (LOC)

capability. Though Grant believed that the balance of losses in the campaign had favored him, in fact, the Confederacy was able to maintain the manpower balance between the armies through the end of 1864. In Lincoln's defense, Lee would have undoubtedly sought to exploit any major shift of Union forces from the Rappahannock to the James, though the president had no way of knowing how uniquely unprepared the Confederacy had been to do that in the spring of 1864.

Lee had long feared a Union seaborne movement to the James because the Confederacy had no means to repel it, nor could the Confederacy hope to prevail should Richmond fall under siege. Since 1862, Lee had successfully executed preemptive offensives, using maneuver and initiative to counter Union advantages in manpower and material. But Davis failed to heed Lee's advice to do so again in 1864, despite having the means available. Had Lee been provided in April or early May with the extra men he actually received in late May and June, the chances of his spoiling Grant's attack or fighting it to a standstill north of Richmond would have been considerably greater.

Historians have long debated the inevitability of the Confederacy's defeat in the Civil War, the point at which its fortunes turned, and the reasons for its downfall. The 1864 duel between Grant and Lee has likewise fueled deliberation over the relative merits of the two iconic generals. Placing military operations within the broader political context shows that the final outcome was far from certain well into 1864. Hard political realities forced Lincoln and Davis to constrain the strategic choices available to Grant and Lee. Neither general was permitted to adopt his preferred course of action, and both were forced to improvise. When battle was joined in May 1864, the decision of victory very much remained to be determined by the trial of war.

Shawn Woodford
is a historian employed
by the Federal government.
He received his Ph.D. in War
Studies from King's College,
University of London,
in 2004. The thoughts and
views expressed here are
entirely his own.

The Battles of the Cold Harbors

APPENDIX B
BY CHRISTIAN E. FEARER

War has often been described as a plague, and on May 31, 1864, it descended for a second time on the rural communities scattered around the New and Old Cold Harbor crossroads of Hanover County, 12 miles northeast of Richmond. Drawn to Old Cold Harbor by the network of roads that converged there, Federal and Confederate forces exchanged the opening shots of what would evolve into a nearly two-week battle. This battle was more often akin to a stalemate, accented by periodically intense fighting with high casualties, limited breakthroughs, and miles of both elaborate, reinforced earthworks and quickly constructed, minimalist entrenchments.

The armies that clashed that final day of May were familiar with the gently rolling fields and woods north and east of the sluggish Chickahominy River. Over some of these same fields and through some of these very woods, elements of the armies battled fiercely two years prior, when, on June 27, 1862, portions of the Army of the Potomac and what would become the Army of Northern Virginia fought the battle of Gaines' Mill, then occasionally referred to—at least before 1864—as the battle of Cold Harbor. Separated by two years, these two battles around the Cold Harbors were profoundly different and reflect significant changes in the character of the broader war, particularly in the East.

A marker sits near the site of New Cold Harbor, "where two battlefields meet"—the 1862 battle of Gaines Mill and the 1864 battle of Cold Harbor. The marker occupies a small island at the intersection of Cold Harbor Road and the road that leads to the Watt house, a prominent feature on the Gaines Mill battlefield. (CM)

In spring 1862, the Confederacy's days appeared numbered. West of the Appalachians, rebel forces surrendered Forts Henry and Donelson; Nashville had fallen to the Federals; Confederates lost the battle of Shiloh; and the Confederacy's largest city, New Orleans, had fallen to Union forces. By May, the largest U.S. army, the Army of the Potomac, marched under

The battlefield at Ganes Mill.
(CM)

the command of Maj. Gen. George B. McClellan up the Virginia Peninsula between the York and James rivers and maneuvered into position east of Richmond, threatening the capital with a possible siege. McClellan's advance was slowed by rain and his near-constant concern for his enemy's perceived numerical superiority, a state of mind that often went beyond prudent caution to paranoia. By the final week of May the muddy roads east of Richmond began to dry and harden, allowing the Federal army to resume its close on the city, defended by an assortment of Confederate commands under Gen. Joseph E. Johnston.

On May 31, elements of both armies clashed at Seven Pines and Fair Oaks. Civilians living in Richmond and hearing the sounds of battle coming from the east rushed to the city's hills and to the tops of the tallest buildings, stretching their necks in hopes of glimpsing the battle that could mean either defeat or deliverance. By evening and after inconclusive fighting, a shell fragment from a nearby explosion struck Johnston, sending him to the ground and then to Richmond to receive medical care. Jefferson Davis turned to Gen. Robert E. Lee, moving the general from his desk assignment in Richmond to field command. Davis' decision was met with skepticism by many throughout the Confederacy, who were concerned by what appeared to be Lee's penchant for entrenching, which earned him the sobriquet "King of Spades." Despite McClellan's insistence that it was his army that fought at a numerical disadvantage, it was the Confederates that were outnumbered. With McClellan's mighty army arranged before Richmond's gates and fed by a supply line running from the army's rear to the Pamunkey River, Lee faced a dilemma. He could either succumb to a siege—all of which to this point in the war had ended in defeat for the South—or he could somehow seize the initiative and force McClellan to abandon his forward positions. Perhaps, thought Lee, he could even defeat and destroy the Army of the Potomac.

Lee's plan was a gamble. He summoned from the Shenandoah Valley Maj. Gen. Thomas "Stonewall" Jackson, whose outnumbered, swift-moving soldiers recently outmarched and outfought their Union counterparts there. With Jackson from the Valley, Lee intended to consolidate his forces against the Federal right positioned near Mechanicsville and separated from the rest of the army by the sluggish Chickahominy, which in that vicinity resembled a swamp more than a river. Leaving a holding force between the Army of the Potomac and Richmond, the brunt of Lee's attack would fall on McClellan's right flank, held by Brig. Gen. Fitz John Porter's V Corps. It was Lee's hope that by threatening the flank and Federal supply line, McClellan would be forced to withdraw at least from his present position if not the Peninsula entirely.

Lee put his plan into action on June 26, when Confederate forces under the command of Maj. Gen. Ambrose Powell Hill attacked the Federal position along Beaver Dam Creek. Intended to be a coordinated attack by forces under Hill, Jackson, and Maj. Gen. James Longstreet, the engagement was instead fought piecemeal and rather easily repulsed. It was not until nightfall that Jackson arrived in the vicinity of the battlefield, and although the Federal V Corps had easily repulsed the previous attacks, Jackson's looming presence forced Union commanders to reconsider their strategy. The following morning, Porter withdrew to a position along Boatswain's Creek near Dr. William Gaines' grist mill, located in the vicinity of New Cold Harbor. From their new positions, Porter's men would fight a holding action, keeping Lee's Confederates at bay and buying time to prepare for either the Army of the Potomac's repositioning or withdrawal.

The V Corps' new position was impressive. Topped by a high, clear plateau covered by artillery, their lines ran nearly one and a half miles, arranged in two parallel lines running along the hillside between the plateau and Boatswain's Creek. With the artillery positioned atop, a line of infantry was positioned midway down the embankment and the other line

Maj. Gen. George McClellan was all spit and polish, and he was beloved by his men. One of his nicknames was "The Young Napoleon" because of his supposed battlefield prowess—which he repeatedly failed to show. (LOC)

nearer the bottom, collectively providing three lines of defense. By early afternoon, the V Corps was in position and watched the Confederates' movements by the clouds of dust kicked up by the columns of soldiers marching down dry roads. Parallel and converging roads allowed the Confederates to consolidate their forces opposite the Federals yet permitted their dispersal along a wide front. On the Federal left, Confederates centered roughly on New Cold Harbor; on the right flank, they formed in the vicinity of Old Cold Harbor. From near those locations, Confederates numbering 60,000 pressed 34,000 Federals over five-and-a-half hours, beginning at around 2:30 p.m. However, their disjointed attacks were repeatedly repulsed.

With daylight fading and his force finally concentrated, Lee ordered a general charge against the Federals. Stretching west of New Cold Harbor to Old Cold Harbor, Confederates emerged from their positions and charged the Federal line. Beginning from positions just west of New Cold Harbor, rebels under the command of Brig. Gen. John Bell Hood pierced the Union line near its left flank, forcing

Federal soldiers up the hillside and fleeing toward the rickety bridges spanning the Chickahominy. Nearly simultaneously, Confederates punctured the Federal right, likewise resulting in its collapse and retreat. Darkness ended the day's fighting and halted the Rebels' pursuit. Confederate victory—Lee's first tactical victory commanding what would, in significant part, become the Army of Northern Virginia—was definitive. Lee held the initiative and, over the next four days, doggedly pursued McClellan, who made for a new base of operation on the James River. After a week of brutal fighting, the bloodied and beaten Army of the Potomac were gone from Richmond's gates. The city was at least temporarily redeemed. Gaines' Mill was Lee's only true tactical victory of the strategically successful Seven Days campaign; the largest battle was also the costliest. In less than six hours 15,000 men fell killed, wounded, or captured. Nearly 9,000 of those casualties were Confederates.

Lt. Gen. Ulysses S. Grant came from the rough-and-tumble West, and the men of the Army of the Potomac reserved judgment on him until he proved himself. One observer referred to him as "the dust-covered man." (LOC)

When the two armies clashed on June 27, it was a standup engagement. While the Federal defenders assumed a mostly static defense, they met their enemy in relatively open order. Had the V Corps entrenched, the result may have been very different and much costlier for Lee. Regardless, destruction at a level unprecedented in the Eastern Theater was left in the battle's wake. The dead—both men and horses—littered the fields and woods, which were converted to cemeteries with graves so shallow that light rains revealed the contents.

The Seven Days saved Richmond, and the fickle pendulum of morale swung once again in the Confederates' favor. Over the next nearly 20 months, fighting would rage in northern Virginia, western Maryland, and central Pennsylvania before the armies once again settled on lines between Washington, D.C, and Richmond. Despite three years of war, the question of Union remained undecided, guaranteeing that fighting would continue into its fourth spring and summer.

Spring 1864 pitted Lee against Ulysses S. Grant, who as general in chief of the Union armies attached himself to Maj. Gen. George G. Meade's Army of the Potomac. Unlike previous years and campaigns, Grant intended to constantly pressure Lee, robbing him of prolonged interludes between engagements, which had previously allowed his army to repair losses in men and materiel. Lee's aggressive tactics and strategic offensives over the previous two years had bled his army. By spring 1864, Lee lost flexibility and realized that he must now rely on a more defensive posture that would preserve his army and inflict heavy Federal losses. If Union casualties were high, then perhaps Northern public opinion would be swayed toward peace, a sentiment that would possibly be expressed in upcoming Northern elections.

Lee's limitations were evident in altered tactics. Gone were the days of mutual open-field battle when and where possible. Instead, the series of battles beginning in May were noted by often-formidable earthworks and relatively fixed Confederate positions. The result was significant casualties for the attacking Federals. By month's end, Grant's shifts east and south brought both armies back to Hanover County. The roads that converged on the Old Cold Harbor crossroads assumed renewed value to both armies. Having escaped the immediate ravages of the Civil War for almost two years, the plague of war returned to Cold Harbor with vengeance.

Although the 1862 and 1864 battlefields did not directly correspond, the southern end of both armies' lines in 1864 did cut across the former battlefield, specifically in the vicinity of the McGhee farm. Grim reminders greeted the soldiers there. Skeletons—some with tattered uniform remnants—were visible, rusted and rotting equipment littered parts of the old battlefield, and grinning skulls peeked from shallow graves.

But while the two battlefields shared common ground, there were few other similarities. Most noticeabe was the change in tactics, which were—and remain—visible on the physical landscape. By the end of June 2, when most of both armies were in position, Confederate engineers oversaw the construction of elaborate earthworks across their front. Although Grant had come to believe that Lee's army was demoralized and weakened leading him to order a general attack of three corps against the Confederates on June 3, the fire that came from these earthworks convincingly affirmed rebel tenacity and ferocity. Only elements of the Federal II Corps successfully penetrated the Confederate line near the McGhee farm on the eastern end of the 1862 battlefield; however, they were unable to exploit their gains. Having attempted to storm the Confederate positions, surviving Federal soldiers along the entire line of advance dug their own set of opposing earthworks and settled in for nine days' worth of sniping and sporadic exchanges of artillery and rifle fire. Finally, on the night of June 12, the Army of the Potomac slipped from its earthworks and disappeared into the darkness once again moving east and then south, this time to Petersburg.

When the Confederates peered across the battlefield on the morning of June 13, they were met by an eerie calm. With the Federal forces gone, Lee claimed yet another tactical victory; however, it was bittersweet for the Confederates. Lee—and undoubtedly many of his men—realized that should Grant slip from Cold Harbor, successfully cross the James, and establish a siege, defeat would likely come in a matter of time. Gaines' Mill—or the first battle of Cold Harbor—resulted in Lee's first tactical victory. The 1864 battle of Cold Harbor was, in hindsight, his last tactical victory in a major, general engagement; despite localized successes, Lee would lose the nearly 10-month siege of Petersburg and ultimately surrendered the remnants of his army at Appomattox. Outright Confederate political defeat was not a foregone conclusion following Cold Harbor, especially with

The dead of Cold Harbor (LOC)

the upcoming election, but if Lincoln retained the presidency, it would prove even more difficult for the Confederates to force final victory. In some ways, Cold Harbor was a gasp for relief. It may have provided the Confederacy with another breath, but the long-term prognosis remained dire.

Since 1862, the war—and its battles—changed significantly. For veterans of Gaines' Mill, the evolution of the war would have been evident when, two years later, they returned to the very fields to fight the battle of Cold Harbor. In the interim, the armies had clashed on battlefields from Virginia to Pennsylvania only to return to the very same place. Any community cast into the crucible of the Civil War could have understandably considered itself cursed; the rural communities near the Cold Harbors were twice cursed. In two years and after two major battles, civilians and the armies that clashed on and over their properties bore witness to the war's evolution, a change clearly visible on the physical landscape.

To this day, rounded remnants of once-formidable earthworks and quickly constructed trenches remain silent reminders of a violent struggle. Meanwhile, the homes and farms that survived these battles remind us of a community's encounter with the ravages of war. Collectively, these artifacts and the accounts of the battles' participants tell a story of tragedy and triumph, of battle and war at crossroads called Cold Harbor.

Christian E. Fearer is a graduate of West Virginia University and a distinguished graduate of the U.S. Naval War College. He has worked with and for the National Park Service in a variety of capacities, including time at Richmond National Battlefield Park.

The Battle at North Anna River

APPENDIX C
BY DONALD C. PFANZ

With terrible clashes at Spotsylvania Court House and Cold Harbor to bookend it, the encounter between the armies along the banks of the North Anna River has often gone overlooked. However, it represented perhaps the greatest lost opportunity for the Army of Northern Virginia during the entire Overland Campaign.

Forced to abandon his elaborate entrenchments around Spotsylvania, Lee chose the North Anna River, 25 miles to the south, as the next spot to make a stand. Holding the North Anna line would enable him to protect the railroads that came together at Hanover Junction—railroads important not just to the welfare of Richmond but to his own army. The river's steep banks would make it hard for Grant to cross and make even harder for him to escape should Lee defeat him. And unlike Fredericksburg, 17 months before, the undulating nature of the ground afforded the Southern commander the prospect of pursuing the enemy across the river, should he defeat him. At the time of the battle of Fredericksburg, Lee had advocated withdrawing to the North Anna, but President Davis would not allow it, wishing to preserve the farmland below the Rappahannock for the Confederacy. Now Lee would get his chance.

The march to the North Anna was fraught with peril for both sides. In order to pry Lee from his Spotsylvania defenses, Grant had sent Maj. Gen. Winfield S. Hancock's II Corps on a 20-mile forced march to Milford Station on the Richmond, Fredericksburg & Potomac Railroad. There, far behind the Confederate army, Hancock was in position to cut Lee's lines of communication with Richmond and directly threaten the Southern capital. But being so distant from the rest of the Union army left Hancock vulnerable, and as soon as Lee showed signs of abandoning his Spotsylvania entrenchments Grant started after him. On May 21 both armies found themselves strung out over a wide area, vulnerable to a quick thrust from the other. Each general was more concerned about the safety of his own army rather than attacking the

The North Anna River is still crossable at Ox Ford, but steep banks on either side made the passage impossible for Federal soldiers because Confederate artillery on the south bank commanded the crossing. (CM)

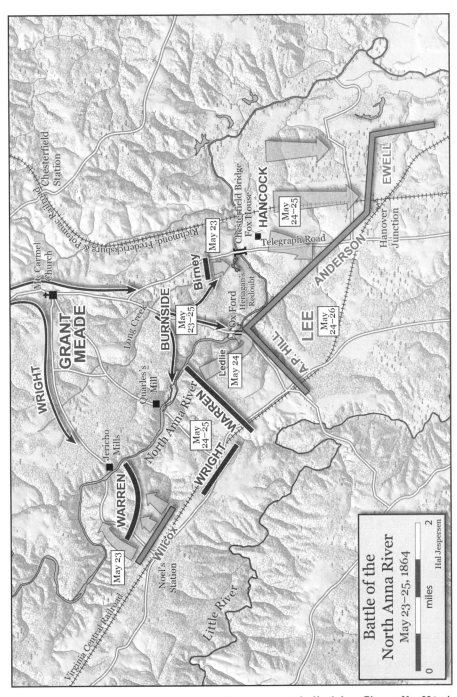

BATTLE OF THE NORTH ANNA RIVER—The Union army's appearance at the North Anna River on May 23 took Lee by surprise. Before he could do anything about it, Barlow's division overran Henegan's Redoubt, north of the river, and Warren's corps gained a foothold south of the river at Jericho Mills. Lee countered by forming his line in the shape of an inverted "V" with its apex at Ox Ford. Grant probed Lee's new line, but only Ledlie's brigade attacked it.

Union troops occupy an abandoned Confederate redoubt at North Anna. (LOC)

enemy, however, and the day passed without either side taking advantage of the unique opportunity to strike the other.

By noon, May 22, the Army of Northern Virginia had crossed the North Anna, again placing itself squarely between the Army of the Potomac and Richmond. Grant now had two options: he could drive directly south and attack Lee's army along the North Anna or he could slide to the east, crossing Pamunkey River (into which the North Anna flowed), and approach Richmond from the northeast. The Pamunkey route offered several advantages, including bringing the army into closer proximity with Maj. Gen. Benjamin Butler's Army of the James, then hemmed in at Bermuda Hundred, south of Richmond, and Maj. Gen. Philip Sheridan's cavalry at White House Landing. Grant, however, chose the bolder (and some would say more foolhardy) course of action: striking Lee at the North Anna. The North Anna option had little to recommend it, but Grant had his adversary on the run and he was determined to keep up the pressure.

Confident that the Union commander would cross farther to the east, at the Pamunkey, Lee took no steps to meet Grant in battle on the North Anna. His troops were resting from their hard march when

Maj. Gen. Winfield Scott Hancock leads the II Corps across the Chesterfield Bridge. (LOC)

the Union army approached the river late on May 23 and began shelling their camps. Lee was standing on the porch of Parson Thomas H. Fox drinking a glass of buttermilk when the bombardment opened and narrowly escaped death when a Union shell slammed into the porch where he was standing. Lee calmly finished his drink and rode off. Minutes later, a second shell struck the chimney of the house, sending an avalanche of bricks crashing down on soldiers below.

As the Confederates scrambled into position along the river, Hancock's corps pushed south toward Chesterfield Bridge, the wooden span that carried the Telegraph Road across the North Anna. A small, three-sided earthen fort built in 1863 stood sentinel over the bridge. In and around the work was Col. John Henegan's South Carolina brigade. Henegan commanded the only Confederate troops still north of the river, and at that moment he and his men felt very much alone, as indeed they were. As the sun began to set, Hancock charged the work, capturing, killing, or wounding 100 of Henegan's men and capturing as many more.

About the same time, Maj. Gen. Gouverneur K. Warren's V Corps was crossing the North Anna four miles upriver, at Jericho Mills. As his divisions passed over the river, Warren formed them into a defensive line covering the crossing. Brigadier

General Samuel W. Crawford's division anchored the left end of Warren's line on the river near the Fontaine house while the divisions of Brig. Gens. Charles Griffin and Lysander Cutler extended the line westward toward another stretch of river on the right. Before Cutler could take up his position, however, the Confederates struck. Warned by Confederate cavalry of the crossing, Lt. Gen. A. P. Hill sent Maj. Gen. Cadmus M. Wilcox's division forward with the intention of either capturing the Federals or driving them into the river. Warren's men were just settling down for dinner when Hill's cannon opened fire on them, shaking the earth with their salvos. Moments later Wilcox's men came charging from the woods, penetrating the gap on Warren's right as yet unfilled by Cutler.

Surprised and outflanked, the Union line began to unravel as panic-stricken soldiers scampered for the safety of the river. Fortunately for Warren, his artillery stood firm. Three batteries on his right poured double-shotted canister into Wilcox's ranks as they struggled to cross a ravine. A Union counterattack, in turn, succeeded in stampeding the Confederates. Wilcox later recalled "the singular spectacle...of two opposing lines giving way at the same time." The Confederates fell back to their starting point at the railroad and awaited attack, but Warren did not pursue. Separated from the rest of the army and with the river to his back, he had no desire to continue a struggle with an enemy of unknown size. Wilcox too was content to let the matter rest. Although reinforced by another division late in the day, he feared that Warren might turn his right flank, severing his connection with the rest of the army. Such caution did not sit well with Lee. Later, during an examination of the ground, Lee chided the commander of his Third Corps saying: "General Hill, why did you let those people cross here? Why didn't you throw your whole force on them and drive them back as Jackson would have done?"

Although Warren's successful crossing of the North Anna thwarted Lee's plans to defend the river, he was still unwilling to relinquish control of the railroad junction to Grant. Instead, he turned the situation to his advantage by anchoring the center of his line at Ox Ford, a particularly strong

Union artillery at North Anna
(LOC)

point on the river, and throwing back the flanks of his army so that his line resembled an inverted "V." The next day, when the two wings of Grant's army advanced, Hancock at Chesterfield Bridge and Warren and Wright at Jericho Mills, they would find the Confederate army between them, protected by strong works of earth and logs. In order for one wing to support the other, Union troops would have to march six miles and cross the river not once, but twice. Lee, by contrast, could easily shuffle troops from one end of the army to the other using his interior lines. Once the Federals had committed themselves, he would mass his army against one wing of the Union army, pinning it against the river, while holding back the other wing with a skeleton force.

Lee had set the perfect trap, and Grant obligingly blundered right into it. Mistaking the lack of resistance at the river as evidence of a Confederate retreat, the Union commander on May 24 ordered the Army of the Potomac across the river in pursuit. But on this day, at least, fortune favored the North. At the moment when Lee should have sprung the trap, he lay prostrate in his tent, incapacitated by illness muttering to himself, "We must strike them a blow. We must never let them pass us again. We must strike them a blow." Belatedly Grant recognized his peril and ordered his troops to entrench. With every spadeful of earth, the crisis abated. The opportunity to cripple the Army of the Potomac passed; Lee would never get another.

Grant misinterpreted Lee's inaction on May 24 as evidence that the Army of Northern Virginia had lost the will to fight. "Lee's army is really whipped," he informed officials in Washington. "The prisoners we now take show it, and the action of his army shows it unmistakably." When Grant left the North Anna River on May 26, he did so convinced that one more attack would shatter Confederate resistance and end the war. He discovered his mistake eight days later at Cold Harbor.

TO REACH NORTH ANNA BATTLEFIELD PARK FROM THE NORTH
(from Fredericksburg, Virginia or Washington D.C.)

From I-95 South, take exit 104 and merge onto Rogers Clark Boulevard (Rt. 207 W) toward Carmel Church. This will bring you to Jefferson Davis Highway (U.S. Rt. 1. Take a left and follow that south for approximately 4.7 miles. After you cross the North Anna River, look for Verdun Road (Rt. 684) on your right. Proceed down this route for approximately 2.5 miles. The entrance to the park will be on your right. Follow corresponding signs to reach the parking area.

TO ARRIVE AT NORTH ANNA BATTLEFIELD PARK FROM THE SOUTH (from Richmond)

From I-95 north, take exit 98 (VA 30 North/Kings Dominion Boulevard). Turn left onto VA-30 North and follow for eight-tenths of a mile. This will bring you to Jefferson Davis Highway (U.S. Rt.1). Make a right here and follow this route north for approximately 1.4 miles. Turn left on Verdun Road (Rt. 684) and follow it approximately 2.5 miles. The entrance to the park will be on your right. The entrance to the park will be on your right. Follow corresponding signs to reach the parking area.

Donald C. Pfanz worked for 32 years as a National Park Service historian, most of it at Fredericksburg and Spotsylvania County National Military Park. He has written several books on the Civil War, and is a co-author of the Emerging Civil War Series title No Turning Back: A Guide to the 1864 Overland Campaign.

Ulysses S. Grant ever-after regretted sending men across this ground.

Cold Harbor in Memory

APPENDIX D

BY CHRIS MACKOWSKI
AND PHILLIP S. GREENWALT

"I have always regretted that the last assault at Cold Harbor was ever made," wrote Ulysses S. Grant in his *Memoirs*.

By the time he wrote of that regret in 1885, he'd had 20 years to reflect on it. Death was very much on his mind. As he wrote his memoirs, he was dying of cancer. The Memoirs, he knew, would survive him and serve as, quite literally, his last word on the Civil War. He took painstaking care to elaborate on most of his battlefield experiences, and yet he wrote almost nothing about Cold Harbor. In the context of those other well-documented engagements, his virtual silence is telling.

Although he didn't write about it, that last charge is the one thing he most remembered for at Cold Harbor—indeed, probably for the entire Overland Campaign. It made perfect fodder for the "Grant the Butcher" mythology that history has saddled him with in the century and a half since.

In less than half an hour, Grant lost as many as seven thousand men.

Seemingly forgotten is the fact that Confederate General Robert E. Lee lost a similar number of men during a similar span of time some 11 months earlier in Gettysburg when he sent portions of his Army of Northern Virginia across a mile of open Pennsylvania farmland.

No one called him "Lee the Butcher" for it, though. Rather, Pickett's Charge is usually remembered as a paragon of Southern valor and manliness, of tragic nobility, of desperate *"If only...."* Lee's charge at Gettysburg has been romanticized in much the same way that Grant's charge at Cold Harbor has been vilified.

Yet one might argue that Lee was, indeed, a butcher—through willful neglect if not outright senseless slaughter. Consider the aftermath of Cold Harbor, when Grant asked for a chance to collect the wounded from the battlefield.

"[H]ereafter when no battle is raging," Grant proposed on June 5, "either party be authorized to send to any point between the pickets or skirmish lines, unarmed men bearing litters." If Lee had something else in mind, Grant said, "any other method equally fair to both parties you may propose for meeting the end desired, will be accepted by me."

A Lee more interested in mercy than in protocol might have acquiesced, but instead, the Southern commander spent days niggling over the wording. "I fear that

Famed photographer Matthew Brady reached the Army of the Potomac when it was ensconced at Cold Harbor. He took a number of photographs of the Union high command. Among them was one of Grant leaning against a tree near his headquarters. It is one of the most iconic photos of the general-in-chief and of the Civil War. (LOC)

such an arrangement will lead to misunderstanding and difficulty," he said. "I propose . . . that when either party desires to remove their dead and wounded, a flag of truce be sent, as is customary."

Grant tried to dodge the issue, but Lee would have none of it. The Confederate commander, steeped in the knowledge of military protocol and honor, would not be duped. "I regret to find that I did not make myself understood in my communication yesterday," he said in a subsequent dispatch. He "could not consent to the burial of the dead and the removal of the wounded . . . in the way you propose, but that when either party desire such permission it shall e asked for by flag of truce in the usual way."

Certainly Lee stood to gain a vital public relations victory by prying such a concession from Grant. To ask for a flag of truce was to admit defeat—and such an admission, for Grant, would have been a devastating cap to a month of unprecedented bloodletting. Grant's campaign had worn down not only Lee's army but the Northern will to wage war, as well. Lee counted on that weakened resolve as his best hope for an eventual peace on Confederate terms.

But that public relations battle resulted in hundreds more casualties as suffering men trapped between the lines finally succumbed to their wounds in the scorching Virginia heat and sweltering humidity with no aid or water or, it seems, mercy. Grant finally caved on June 7. The condition of the wounded, "suffering from want of attention . . . compels me to ask for a suspension of hostilities," he wrote.

By then, as one Union soldier lamented, it was too late for most of the wounded men: "It is dreadful to think of those others whom nursing might have saved, yet who died in bitterness and agony and were buried among the heaps of unrecognized dead."

Perhaps Grant was just as much to blame because he could have acquiesced to Lee's demands sooner, but as the commander who first extended the olive branch, Grant demonstrated a degree of compassion that Lee did not. That hardly reconciles with any "Grant the Butcher" mythology.

Grant launched that assault on June 3 after a string of successes against the Confederate army. Although stymied in the Wilderness and at Spotsylvania, and despite a nearly catastrophic mistake at the North Anna, Grant and his army began to get their feet under themselves as they crossed the Pamunkey, pushed through Haw's Shop, put the squeeze on at Totopotomoy, and scored successes at Bethesda Church and the road to Cold Harbor. Then on June 1, his army not only held off Confederates but scored moderate gains. Confederate deserters had already convinced him after North Anna that Lee's army was whipped, and Lee's inability to stop his inexorable march south and east seemed to reinforce that impression.

Grant planned his June 3 attack, then, with plenty of reason to believe he could achieve victory. He also had all of June 2 to arrange his forces exactly as he wanted them. "I may be mistaken, but I feel that our success over Lee's army is already assured," he confided to Washington.

But as the old military adage goes, "No plan survives contact with the enemy," and so it went for Grant. His men assaulted in vain—and in doing so, erased all the smaller successes he'd achieved at Cold Harbor up until that point. He is remembered only for "the last assault."

Lost Cause writers in the early years were quick to focus on Grant's failed assault because it allowed them to divert attention to the most inconvenient salient fact of all: Grant was on the doorstep of Richmond when he ordered that assault, despite the best efforts of Lee's army to stop his advance. Sure, he lost the battle that day, but he was winning the campaign.

The pro-Southern interpretation of events, accepted as conventional wisdom for so long, was enshrined on the battlefield itself in the 1920s by the Battlefield Markers Association, which recruited the great Southern historian Douglas Southall Freeman to write text for some 56 markers—text that was then cast in iron and set on squat granite pedestals for automobile travelers to read as they toured the battlefields.

The public relations battle at Cold Harbor lasted well into the twentieth century, but by then, it was as one-sided as the June 3 battle, especially with Grant's memoirs so silent on the affair.

Grant always regretted that last assault, but had he known how the battle for memory would play out, perhaps his greater regret would have been that he hadn't said more.

Historian Douglas Southall Freeman, who wrote and raised money for many of the roadside markers featured in this book, did much to influence the public's understanding about Grant. He is buried in Richmond's Hollywood Cemetery among the Confederate dead he so lionized in his work. (CM)

Chris Mackowski, Ph.D., is a co-founder of Emerging Civil War and, with Kristopher White, co-author of a number of books about the war. He is a writing professor at St. Bonaventure University.

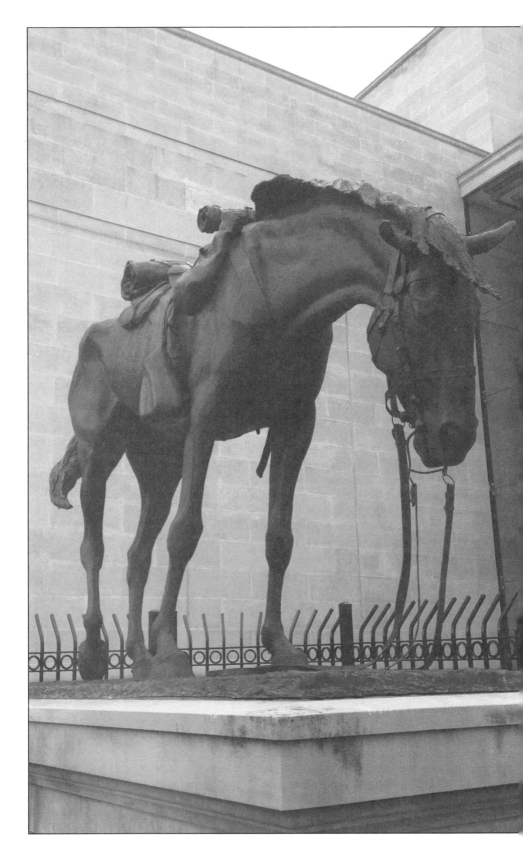

"On to Richmond!"

APPENDIX E
BY PHILLIP S. GREENWALT
AND CHRIS MACKOWSKI

For four years in the American Civil War, Richmond was the grand prize for the Union armies. Thousands of blue-coated Union soldiers took up the simple war cry: "On to Richmond!"

Robert E. Lee's response was typical: "Richmond must not be given up; it shall not be given up!"

Now Richmond is one of the epicenters for remembering this tragic conflict, and the former capital of the Confederacy beckons visitors with a plethora of historic sites to investigate.

HOLLYWOOD CEMETERY (*412 S. Cherry St.*)
Opened in 1849, Hollywood Cemetery overlooks the James River. More than 25 Confederate generals are buried there, including J. E. B. Stuart, Fitzhugh Lee, and George Pickett, as well as Confederate President Jefferson Davis and U.S. Presidents James Monroe and John Tyler. Also included among the number of former Confederates that lay there are remains of those who fell during Pickett's Charge on July 3, 1863. Other notables include Dr. Hunter Holmes McGuire, Stonewall's Jackson's surgeon; Matthew Fontaine Maury, the father of modern oceanography; and Douglas Southall Freeman, the noted Southern historian.

The James River from Hollywood Cemetery (CM)

A memorial to the 1.5 million horses and mules who were killed, wounded, or died of disease during the Civil War stands in front of the Virginia Historical Society. The bronze statue, dedicated in 1997, was sculpted by Tessa Pullan. *(428 North Boulevard)* (CM)

Monument Avenue

Monuments to Robert E. Lee, "Stonewall" Jackson, J. E. B. Stuart (left), Davis, and Maury sit along one of the city's most picturesque streets. In 1887, city plans were drawn up

that included proposed sites to create a grand avenue extending west past the end of an already upscale locale. The first monument installed, Lee's, was dedicated on May 29, 1890; more than one-hundred thousand people attended the unveiling. In the early 20th century, private residences and buildings began to grace the thoroughfare. In 1907, Stuart and Jackson joined Lee in monument form, followed in 1919 by Davis. Maury completed the early 20th century dedications when his statue was unveiled in 1929. A statue to Arthur Ashe, a great tennis player from Richmond, was added to Monument Avenue in 1996.

Jeb Stuart on Monument Drive (CM)

Historic Tredegar *(500 Tredegar St.)*

The American Civil War Center and the main visitor center for the Richmond National Battlefield Park both sit on the site of the former Tredegar Iron Works. Created in 1936, Richmond National Battlefield Park now preserves 7,307 acres of American History— over 30 associated Civil War sites in 13 units. Take in the sites of this large industrial complex that churned out small arms and artillery tubes for the Confederate military. Richmond National Battlefield also preserves a medical museum at Chimborazo *(3215 East Broad St.)*, one of the largest wartime hospitals run by the Confederacy, also located in downtown Richmond.

Historic Tredegar (above) and the Chimborazo Medical Museum (left) (PG)

THE MUSEUM OF THE CONFEDERACY
AND THE WHITE HOUSE OF THE CONFEDERACY

(1201 E Clay St.)

Unfortunately, both buildings are buried within the now-sprawling Virginia Commonwealth University Medical campus. The White House of the Confederacy was the former home of Jefferson Davis. Sitting adjacent to it, the Museum of the Confederacy contains the largest collection of Confederate memorabilia in the country, including such iconic pieces as Robert E. Lee's surrender sword from Appomattox, the first "Stainless Banner" national flag, and J. E. B. Stuart's plumed hat.

Ironically, the White House of the Confederacy is actually gray. (PG)

CONFEDERATE SOLDIERS AND SAILORS MONUMENT

Located in Libby's Hill Park in the Church Hill section of Richmond, the monument was dedicated on May 30, 1894 at a reunion of Confederate veterans. William L. Sheppard designed the 73-foot high column after Pompey's Pillar in Egypt. Gracing the top of the column is a 17-foot high Confederate soldier.

Confederate Soldiers and Sailors Monument (PG)

The Virginia state capitol building also served as the Confederate capitol. (PG)

THE VIRGINIA STATE CAPITOL *(1000 Bank St.)*

Thomas Jefferson designed the state capitol building, modeling it off a Roman temple in France. Several statues sit on the grounds, including a massive statue of George Washington and smaller statues of Stonewall Jackson, Dr. Hunter McGuire, and former governor and Civil War general "Extra Billy" Smith. There's also a Civil Rights memorial.

George Washington (right), "Extra Billy" Smith (bottom, left), Stonewall Jackson (center), and Dr. Hunter McGuire are among the statues that adorn state capitol grounds. (PG/CM/CM/CM)

THE JOHN MARSHALL HOUSE *(818 East Marshall St.)*

For a trip further back in time.... The home of John Marshall, one of the greatest Supreme Court justices, dates to 1790. He and his wife, Poly, lived there until the justice's death in 1835. Preservationists saved the house from destruction after the Marshall family sold it to the City of Richmond in 1911. It now sits on the National and Virginia Historic Registers.

The John
Marshall House
(PG)

THE MAGGIE WALKER HOUSE *(600 North 2nd St.)*

For a trip a little closer in time.... This national historic site was once the home of Civil Rights pioneer Maggie Walker. As a bank president, newspaper editor, and civic leader, Walker advocated educational and economic opportunities for minorities.

The Maggie
Walker House (PG)

THE POE MUSEUM *(16 East Main St.)*

Heralded as "the world's finest collection of Edgar Allan Poe's letters, first editions, memorabilia, and personal belongings," the Poe Museum is located in the oldest house still standing in Richmond (built circa 1737 by Jacob Ege). In 1924, it was placed in the custody of the Poe Shrine (now the Poe Foundation).

The Poe Museum
(PG)

Poe lived in Richmond on and off for his entire life. Although he never actually lived in the building that houses the Poe Museum, it's located just blocks away from his first home and from the offices of the Southern Literary Messenger, where Poe worked as a magazine writer.

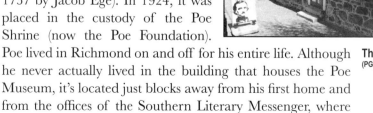

BATTLE OF COLD HARBOR

UNION ORDER OF BATTLE
Lt. Gen. Ulysses S. Grant, General in Chief

ARMY OF THE POTOMAC Maj. Gen. George G. Meade

SECOND CORPS Maj. Gen. Winfield Scott Hancock
First Division Brig. Gen. Francis C. Barlow
First Brigade Col. Nelson A. Miles
26th Michigan • 5th New Hampshire[1] • 2nd New York Heavy Artillery
61st New York • 81st Pennsylvania • 140th Pennsylvania
183rd Pennsylvania

Second Brigade Col. Richard Byrnes[2], Col. Patrick Kelly
28th Massachusetts • 63rd New York • 69th New York • 88th New York
116th Pennsylvania

Third Brigade Col. Clinton D. MacDougall
39th New York • 52nd New York • 57th New York • 111th New York
125th New York • 126th New York

Fourth Brigade Col. John R. Brooke[3], Col. Orlando Morris[4], Col. Lewis
Morris[5]
2nd Delaware • 7th New York Heavy Artillery • 64th New York
53rd Pennsylvania • 145th Pennsylvania•148th Pennsylvania

Second Division Brig. Gen. John Gibbon
First Brigade Col. H. Boyd McKeen[6], Col. Frank Haskell[7]
19th Maine• 1st Co. Sharpshooters • 15th Massachusetts
19th Massachusetts • 20th Massachusetts • 7th Michigan
42nd New York • 59th New York • 82nd New York (2nd Militia)
184th Pennsylvania • 36th Wisconsin

---

1   Arrived as reinforcements on June 1.
2   Killed on June 3.
3   Wounded on June 3.
4   Killed on June 3.
5   Killed on June 4.
6   Killed on June 3.
7   Killed on June 3.

Second Brigade Brig. Gen. Joshua T. Owen
152nd New York • 69th Pennsylvania • 71st Pennsylvania
72nd Pennsylvania • 106th Pennsylvania

Third Brigade Col. Thomas A. Smyth
14th Connecticut • 1st Delaware • 14th Indiana • 12th New Jersey
10th New York Battalion • 108th New York • 4th Ohio•8th Ohio
7th West Virginia

Fourth Brigade Brig. Gen. Robert O. Tyler[8]
8th New York Heavy Artillery • 155th New York • 164th New York
170th New York • 182nd New York

Third Division Maj. Gen. David B. Birney
First Brigade Col. Thomas W. Egan
20th Indiana • 3rd Maine • 40th New York • 86th New York
124th New York • 99th Pennsylvania • 110th Pennsylvania
141st Pennsylvania • 2nd U.S. Sharpshooters

Second Brigade Col. Thomas R. Tannatt
4th Maine • 17th Maine • 3rd Michigan • 5th Michigan
93rd New York • 57th Pennsylvania • 63rd Pennsylvania
105th Pennsylvania • 1st U.S. Sharpshooters

Third Brigade Brig. Gen. Gershom Mott
1st Maine Heavy Artillery • 16th Massachusetts • 5th New Jersey
6th New Jersey • 7th New Jersey • 8th New Jersey • 11th New Jersey
26th Pennsylvania • 115th Pennsylvania

Fourth Brigade Col. William R. Brewster
11th Massachusetts • 70th New York • 71st New York • 73rd New York
74th New York • 120th New York • 84th Pennsylvania

Artillery Col. John C. Tidball
Battery F, 6th Maine Light • 10 Massachusetts Light
1st New Hampshire Light • Battery B, 1st New Jersey Light
Battery G, 1st New York Light • 4th New York Heavy, 3rd Battalion
11th New York Light • 12th New York Light Battery F, 1st Pennsylvania Light
• Batteries A and B, 1st Rhode Island Light
Battery K, 4th United States • Batteries C and I, 5th United States

---

8   Wounded on June 3.

FIFTH CORPS Maj. Gen. Governeur K. Warren
First Division Brig. Gen. Charles Griffin
First Brigade Brig. Romeyn B. Ayres
5th New York[9] • 140th New York • 146th New York
21st Pennsylvania Cavalry (dismounted)[10] • 91st Pennsylvania
155th Pennsylvania • 2nd United States (Companies B, C, F, H, I, K)
11th United States (Companies B, C, D, F, G, 1st Battalion)
12th United States (Companies A, B, C, D, G) • 12th United States
(Companies A, C, D, F, H, 2nd Battalion) • 14th United States, 1st Battalion
17th United States (Companies A, C, D, G, H, 1st Battalion)
17th United States (Companies A, B, C, 2nd Battalion)

Second Brigade Col. Jacob B. Sweitzer
9th Massachusetts • 22nd Massachusetts • 32nd Massachusetts
4th Michigan • 62nd Pennsylvania

Third Brigade Brig. Gen. Joseph J. Bartlett
20th Maine • 18th Massachusetts • 1st Michigan • 16th Michigan
44th New York • 83rd Pennsylvania • 118th Pennsylvania

Second Division Brig. Gen. Henry H. Lockwood[11], Brig. Gen. Samuel
Crawford
First Brigade Col. Peter Lyle
16th Maine • 13th Massachusetts • 39th Massachusetts • 104th New York
90th Pennsylvania•107th Pennsylvania

Second Brigade Col. James L. Bates
12th Massachusetts • 83rd New York • 97th New York • 11th Pennsylvania
88th Pennsylvania

Third Brigade Col. Nathan D. Dushane
1st Maryland • 4th Maryland • 7th Maryland • 8th Maryland
Purnell Legion (Infantry)

Third Division Brig. Gen. Samuel Crawford[12]
First Brigade Col. Martin Hardin
1st Pennsylvania Reserves • 2nd Pennsylvania Reserves
6th Pennsylvania Reserves • 7th Pennsylvania Reserves
11th Pennsylvania Reserves • 13th Pennsylvania Reserves

Third Brigade Col. Joseph W. Fisher
5th Pennsylvania Reserves • 10th Pennsylvania Reserves • 12th Pennsylvania Reserves

---

9   Arrived as reinforcements on June 1.
10   Arrived as reinforcements on June 1.
11   Removed from command on June 2.
12   The division's second brigade was broken up and transferred to the Fifth Corps to
help form the corps' second division.

Independent Brigade Col. J. Howard Kitching
6th New York Heavy Artillery • 15th New York Heavy Artillery

Fourth Division Brig. Gen. Lysander Cutler
First Brigade Col. William W. Robinson
7th Indiana • 19th Indiana • 24th Michigan • 1st Battalion, New York
Sharpshooters • 2nd Wisconsin • 6th Wisconsin • 7th Wisconsin

Second Brigade Col. J. William Hofmann
3rd Delaware • 4th Delaware[13] • 46th New York • 76th New York
95th New York • 147th New York • 56th Pennsylvania • 157th Pennsylvania[14]

Third Brigade Col. Edward S. Bragg
121st Pennsylvania • 142nd Pennsylvania • 143rd Pennsylvania
149th Pennsylvania • 150th Pennsylvania

Artillery Col. Charles S. Wainwright
Battery C, 3rd Massachusetts Light • Battery E, 5th Massachusetts Light
9th Massachusetts Light • Batteries B, C, D, E H & L, 1st New York Light
5th New York Light • 15th New York Light • Battery B, 1st Pennsylvania
Light • Battery B, 4th United States • Battery D, 5th United States

SIXTH CORPS Maj. Gen. Horatio Wright
First Division Brig. Gen. David A. Russell
First Brigade Col. William H. Penrose
1st New Jersey • 2nd New Jersey • 3rd New Jersey • 4th New Jersey
10th New Jersey • 15th New Jersey

Second Brigade Brig. Gen. Emory Upton
5th Maine • 121st New York • 95th Pennsylvania • 96th Pennsylvania
2nd Connecticut Heavy Artillery

Third Brigade Brig. Gen. Henry Eustis
6th Maine • 49th Pennsylvania • 119th Pennsylvania • 5th Wisconsin

Fourth Brigade Col. Nelson Cross
65th New York • 67th New York • 122nd New York • 23rd Pennsylvania
82nd Pennsylvania

Second Division Brig. Gen. Thomas H. Neill
First Brigade Brig. Gen. Frank Wheaton
62nd New York • 93rd Pennsylvania • 98th Pennsylvania
102nd Pennsylvania • 139th Pennsylvania

---

13   Arrived as reinforcements on June 1.
14   Arrived as reinforcements on June 1.

Second Brigade Brig. Gen. Lewis A. Grant
11th Vermont Heavy Artillery • 2nd Vermont • 3rd Vermont
4th Vermont • 5th Vermont • 6th Vermont

Third Brigade Brig. Gen. Daniel D. Bidwell
7th Maine • 43rd New York • 49th New York • 77th New York
61st Pennsylvania

Third Division Brig. Gen. James B. Ricketts
First Brigade Col. William S. Truex[15], Col. John W. Schall[16]
14th New Jersey • 106th New York • 151st New York • 87th Pennsylvania
10th Vermont

Second Brigade Col. Benjamin F. Smith
6th Maryland • 9th New York Heavy Artillery • 110th Ohio
122nd Ohio • 126th Ohio • 67th Pennsylvania • 138th Pennsylvania

Artillery Col. Charles H. Tompkins
Battery D, 4th Maine Light • Battery E, 5th Maine Light • Battery A, 1st
Massachusetts Light • Battery A, 1st New Jersey Light • 1st New York Light
3rd New York Light • 4th New York Heavy, 1st Battalion • Battery H, 1st
Ohio Light • Batteries C, E, G 1st Rhode Island Light • Battery E & M,
5th United States

NINTH CORPS Maj. Gen. Ambrose Burnside
First Division Maj. Gen. Thomas L. Crittenden
First Brigade Brig. Gen. James Ledlie
35th Massachusetts • 56th Massachusetts • 57th Massachusetts
59th Massachusetts • 4th United States • 10th United States

Second Brigade Col. Joseph M. Sudsburg
3rd Maryland • 21st Massachusetts • 100th Pennsylvania

Provisional Brigade Col. Elisha G. Marshall
2nd New York Mounted Rifles (dismounted) • 14th New York Heavy Artillery
24th New York Cavalry (dismounted) • 2nd Pennsylvania Provisional Heavy Artillery

Artillery
Battery B, 2nd Maine Light•14th Massachusetts Battery

Second Division Brig. Gen. Robert B. Potter
First Brigade Col. John Curtin
36th Massachusetts • 58th Massachusetts • 51st New York
45th Pennsylvania • 48th Pennsylvania • 7th Rhode Island

---

15   Wounded on June 1.
16   Wounded on June 1 and June 3.

Second Brigade Col. Simon Griffin
31st Maine • 32nd Maine • 6th New Hampshire • 9th New Hampshire
11th New Hampshire • 17th Vermont

Artillery
11th Massachusetts Battery • 19th New York Battery

Third Division Brig. Gen. Orlando B. Willcox
First Brigade Col. John F. Hartranft
2nd Michigan • 8th Michigan • 17th Michigan • 27th Michigan
109th New York • 51st Pennsylvania

Second Brigade Col. William Humphrey
1st Michigan Sharpshooters • 20th Michigan • 60th Ohio
50th Pennsylvania

Artillery
Battery G, 7th Maine Light • 34th New York Battery

Fourth Division Brig. Gen. Edward Ferrero
First Brigade Col. Joseph K. Sigfried
27th United States Colored Troops • 30th United States Colored Troops
39th United States Colored Troops • 43rd United States Colored Troops

Second Brigade Col. Henry G. Thomas
19th United States Colored Troops • 23rd United States Colored Troops
31st United States Colored Troops

Artillery
Battery D, Pennsylvania Independent • 3rd Vermont Battery

CAVALRY CORPS Maj. Gen. Philip H. Sheridan
First Division Maj. Gen. Alfred T.A. Torbert
First Brigade Brig. Gen. George A. Custer
1st Michigan • 5th Michigan • 6th Michigan • 7th Michigan

Second Brigade Col. Thomas C. Devin
4th New York • 6th New York • 9th New York • 17th Pennsylvania

Reserve Brigade Brig. Gen. Wesley Merritt
19th New York (1st Dragoons) • 6th Pennsylvania • 1st United States
5th United States • 6th United States

Second Division Brig. Gen. David M. Gregg
First Brigade Brig. Gen. Henry E. Davies, Jr.
1st Massachusetts • 1st New Jersey • 10th New York • 6th Ohio
1st Pennsylvania

Second Brigade Col. J. Irvin Gregg
1st Maine • 2nd Pennsylvania• 4th Pennsylvania • 8th Pennsylvania
13th Pennsylvania•16th Pennsylvania

Third Division Brig. Gen. James H. Wilson
First Brigade Col. John B. McIntosh
1st Connecticut • 3rd New Jersey • 2nd New York • 5th New York
2nd Ohio • 18th Pennsylvania

Second Brigade Col. George Chapman
3rd Indiana • 8th New York • 1st Vermont •

Horse Artillery
First Brigade Capt. James M. Robertson
6th New York Battery • Batteries B, D, L, M 2nd United States
Battery A, C, E 4th United States

Second Brigade Capt. Dunbar Ransom
Batteries E, G, H, I, K 1st United States • Battery A, 2nd United States

EIGHTEENTH CORPS Maj. Gen. William F. "Baldy" Smith[17]
First Division Brig. Gen. William T.H. Brooks
First Brigade Brig. Gen. Gilman Marston
81st New York • 96th New York • 98th New York • 139th New York

Second Brigade Brig. Gen. Hiram Burnham
8th Connecticut • 10th New Hampshire • 13th New Hampshire
118th New York

Third Brigade Col. Guy Henry
21st Connecticut • 40th Massachusetts • 92nd New York
58th Pennsylvania • 188th Pennsylvania

Artillery Brigade Capt. Samuel S. Elder
Battery B, 1st United States • Battery L, 4th United States
Battery A, 5th United States

Second Division Brig. Gen. John H. Martindale
First Brigade Brig. Gen. George J. Stannard
23rd Massachusetts • 25th Massachusetts • 27th Massachusetts
9th New Jersey • 55th Pennsylvania

Second Brigade Col. Griffin A. Stedman
11th Connecticut • 8th Maine • 2nd New Hampshire
12th New Hampshire • 148th New York

---

17   Detached from the Army of the James, Maj. Gen. Benjamin Butler commanding.

Third Division Brig. Gen. Charles Devens, Jr.
First Brigade Col. William B. Barton
47th New York • 48th New York • 115th New York • 76th Pennsylvania

Second Brigade Col. Jeremiah Drake[18], Col. Zina Robinson
13th Indiana • 9th Maine • 112th New York • 169th New York

Third Brigade Brig. Gen. Adelbert Ames
4th New Hampshire • 3rd New York • 117th New York
142nd New York • 97th Pennsylvania

---

18   Killed on June 1.

* * *

CONFEDERATE ORDER OF BATTLE
ARMY OF NORTHERN VIRGINIA Gen. Robert E. Lee

FIRST CORPS Maj. Gen. Richard H. Anderson
Kershaw's Division Brig. Gen. Joseph B. Kershaw
Kershaw's Brigade Col. John W. Henagan[1], Col. Lawrence M. Keitt,
Col. John W. Henagan
2nd South Carolina • 3rd South Carolina • 7th South Carolina
8th South Carolina • 15th South Carolina • 20th South Carolina
3rd South Carolina Battalion

Humphrey's Brigade Brig. Gen. Benjamin G. Humphreys
13th Mississippi • 17th Mississippi • 18th Mississippi • 21st Mississippi

Wofford's Brigade Brig. Gen. William T. Wofford
16th Georgia • 18th Georgia • 24th Georgia • Cobb's (Georgia) Legion
Phillips (Georgia) Legion • 3rd Georgia Battalion Sharpshooters

Bryan's Brigade Brig. Gen. Goode Bryan
10th Georgia • 50th Georgia • 51st Georgia • 53rd Georgia

Field's Division Maj. Gen. Charles W. Field
Jenkins' Brigade Col. John Bratton
1st South Carolina • 2nd South Carolina • 5th South Carolina
6th South Carolina • Palmetto Sharpshooters

Gregg's Brigade Brig. Gen. John Gregg
3rd Arkansas • 1st Texas • 4th Texas • 5th Texas

---

1   Replaced by Colonel Keitt from May 31 until Keitt's mortal wounding on June 1.

Law's Brigade Brig. Gen. Evander McIver Law
4th Alabama • 15th Alabama • 44th Alabama • 47th Alabama
48th Alabama

Anderson's Brigade Brig. Gen. George T. Anderson
7th Georgia • 8th Georgia • 9th Georgia • 11th Georgia • 59th Georgia

Benning's Brigade Col. Dudley M. DuBose
2nd Georgia • 15th Georgia • 17th Georgia • 20th Georgia

Pickett's Division Maj. Gen. George E. Pickett
Kemper's Brigade Brig. Gen. William R. Terry
1st Virginia • 3rd Virginia • 7th Virginia • 11th Virginia • 24th Virginia

Hunton's Brigade Brig. Gen. Eppa Hunton
8th Virginia • 19th Virginia • 25th Virginia Battalion (City Battalion)
32nd Virginia • 56th Virginia • 42nd Virginia Cavalry Battalion

Barton's Brigade Brig. Gen. Seth M. Barton
9th Virginia • 14th Virginia • 38th Virginia • 53rd Virginia • 57th Virginia

Corse's Brigade Brig. Gen. Montgomery D. Corse
15th Virginia • 17th Virginia • 18th Virginia • 29th Virginia • 30th Virginia

Hoke's Brigade Lt. Col. William G. Lewis
6th North Carolina • 21st North Carolina • 54th North Carolina
57th North Carolina • 1st North Carolina Battalion

Artillery Brig. Gen. E. Porter Alexander
Haskell's Battalion Maj. John C. Haskell
Flanner's (North Carolina) Battery • Garden's (South Carolina) Battery
Lamkin's (Virginia) Battery • Ramsay's (North Carolina) Battery

Huger's Battalion Lt. Col. Frank Huger
Fickling's (South Carolina) Battery • Moody's (Louisiana) Battery
Parker's (Virginia) Battery • Smith's (Virginia) Battery
Taylor's (Virginia) Battery • Woolfolk's (Virginia) Battery

Cabell's Battalion Col. Henry C. Cabell
Callaway's (Georgia) Battery • Carlton's (Georgia) Battery
McCarthy's (Virginia) Battery • Manly's (North Carolina) Battery

SECOND CORPS Lt. Gen. Richard S. Ewell,[2] Maj. Gen. Jubal A. Early
Ramseur's Division Maj. Gen. Stephen D. Ramseur
Pegram's Brigade Col. Edward Willis,[3] Col. John S. Hoffman
13th Virginia • 31st Virginia • 49th Virginia • 52nd Virginia • 58th Virginia

2   Replaced by Maj. Gen. Jubal A. Early on May 27.
3   Mortally wounded on May 30.

Johnston's Brigade Col. Thomas F. Toon
5th North Carolina • 12th North Carolina • 20th North Carolina
23rd North Carolina

Gordon's Division Maj. Gen. John B. Gordon
Evans's Brigade Brig. Gen. Clement A. Evans
13th Georgia • 26th Georgia • 31st Georgia • 38th Georgia
60th Georgia • 61st Georgia • 12th Georgia Battalion

Louisiana Brigade Col. Zebulon York
1st Louisiana • 2nd Louisiana • 5th Louisiana • 6th Louisiana
7th Louisiana • 8th Louisiana • 9th Louisiana • 10th Louisiana
14th Louisiana • 15th Louisiana

Terry's Brigade Brig. Gen. William Terry
2nd Virginia • 4th Virginia • 5th Virginia • 10th Virginia • 21st Virginia
23rd Virginia • 25th Virginia • 27th Virginia • 33rd Virginia
37th Virginia • 42nd Virginia • 44th Virginia • 48th Virginia • 50th Virginia

Rodes' Division Maj. Gen. Robert E. Rodes
Daniel's Brigade Brig. Gen. Bryan Grimes
32nd North Carolina • 43rd North Carolina • 45th North Carolina
53rd North Carolina • 2nd North Carolina Battaltion

Ramseur's Brigade Col. Risden T. Bennett
1st North Carolina • 2nd North Carolina • 3rd North Carolina
4th North Carolina • 14th North Carolina • 30th North Carolina

Battle's Brigade Brig. Gen. Cullen A. Battle
3rd Alabama • 5th Alabama • 6th Alabama • 12th Alabama
26th Alabama • 61st Alabama

Doles' Brigade Brig. Gen. George Doles,[4] Col. Philip Cooke
4th Georgia • 12th Georgia • 44th Georgia

Artillery Brig. Gen. Armistead L. Long
Braxton's Battalion Lt. Col. Carter M. Braxton
Carpenter's (Virginia) Battery • Cooper's (Virginia) Battery
Hardwicke's (Virginia) Battery

Nelson's Battalion Lt. Col. William Nelson
Kilpatrick's (Virginia) Battery • Massie's (Virginia) Battery
Milledge's (Georgia) Battery

---

4   Killed June 2.

Page's Battalion Maj. Richard C. M. Page
W. P. Carter's (Virginia) Battery • Fry's (Virginia) Battery
Page's (Virginia) Battery • Reese's (Virginia) Battery

Cutshaw's Battalion Maj. Wilfred E. Cutshaw
Carrington's (Virginia) Battery • W. Garber's (Virginia) Battery
Tanner's (Virginia) Battery

Hardaway's Battalion Lt. Col. Robert A. Hardaway
Dance's (Virginia) Battery • Graham's (Virginia) Battery
B. Griffin's (Virginia) Battery • Jones's (Virginia) Battery
B.H. Smith's (Virginia) Battery

THIRD CORPS Lt. Gen. A. P. Hill
Mahone's Division Brig. Gen. William Mahone
Sanders's Brigade Col. John C.C. Sanders
8th Alabama • 9th Alabama • 10th Alabama • 11th Alabama
14th Alabama

Mahone's Brigade Col. David A. Weisiger
6th Virginia • 12th Virginia • 16th Virginia • 41st Virginia
61st Virginia

Harris's Brigade Brig. Gen. Nathaniel II. Harris
12th Mississippi • 16th Mississippi • 19th Mississippi • 48th Mississippi

Finegan's Brigade Brig. Gen. Joseph Finnegan
2nd Florida • 5th Florida • 8th Florida • 9th Florida • 10th Florida •
11th Florida

Wright's Brigade Brig. Gen. Ambrose R. Wright
3rd Georgia • 22nd Georgia • 48th Georgia • 2nd Georgia Battalion
10th Georgia Battalion

Heth's Division Maj. Gen. Henry Heth
Davis's Brigade Brig. Gen. Joseph R. Davis
2nd Mississippi • 11th Mississippi • 26th Mississippi • 42nd Mississippi
55th North Carolina

Cooke's Brigade Brig. Gen. John R. Cooke
15th North Carolina • 27th North Carolina • 46th North Carolina
48th North Carolina

Walker's Brigade Brig. Gen. Birtkett D. Fry
40th Virginia • 47th Virginia • 55th Virginia • 22nd Virginia Battalion
13th Alabama • 1st Tennessee (Provisional) • 7th Tennessee • 14th Tennessee

Kirkland's Brigade Brig. Gen. William W. Kirkland,[5] Col. George H. Faribault
11th North Carolina • 26th North Carolina • 44th North Carolina 47th North Carolina • 52nd North Carolina

Wilcox's Division Maj. Gen. Cadmus M. Wilcox
Lane's Brigade Brig. Gen. James H. Lane,[6] Col. John D. Barry
7th North Carolina • 18th North Carolina • 28th North Carolina 33rd North Carolina • 37th North Carolina

McGowan's Brigade Lt. Col. J. F. Hunt
1st South Carolina (Provisional) • 12th South Carolina • 13th South Carolina • 14th South Carolina • 1st South Carolina (Orr's Rifles)

Scales' Brigade Brig. Gen. Alfred M. Scales,[7] Col. William L. Lowrance
13th North Carolina • 16th North Carolina • 22nd North Carolina 34th North Carolina • 38th North Carolina

Artillery Col. R. Lindsay Walker
Poague's Battalion Lt. Col. William T. Poague
Richard's (Mississippi) Battery • Utterback's (Virginia) Battery Williams' (North Carolina) Battery • Wyatt's (Virginia) Battery

Pegram's Battalion Lt. Col. William J. Pegram
Brander's (Virginia) Battery • Cayce's (Virginia) Battery Ellet's (Virginia) Battery • Marye's (Virginia) Battery Zimmerman's (South Carolina) Battery

McIntosh's Battalion Lt. Col. David G. McIntosh
Clutter's (Virginia) Battery • Donald's (Virginia) Battery Hurt's (Alabama) Battery • Price's (Virginia) Battery

Richardson's Battalion Lt. Col. Charles Richardson
Grandy's (Virginia) Battery • Landry's (Louisiana) Battery Moore's (Virginia) Battery • Penick's (Virginia) Battery

INDEPENDENT COMMAND UNITS SERVING WITH ARMY OF NORTHERN VIRGINIA
Breckenridge's Division Maj. Gen. John C. Breckenridge
Echol's Brigade Brig. Gen. John Echols,[8] Col. George S. Patton
22nd Virginia • 23rd Virginia Battalion • 26th Virginia Battalion

---

5   Wounded June 2.
6   Wounded June 2.
7   Was sick throughout campaign.
8   Temporarily replaced by Col. George S. Patton on May 30.

Wharton's Brigade Brig. Gen. Gabriel C. Wharton
30th Virginia Battalion • 51st Virginia • 62nd Virginia (Mounted)

Maryland Line Col. Bradley T. Johnson
2nd Maryland[9] • 1st Maryland Cavalry[10] • 1st Maryland Battery
2nd Maryland Battery • 4th Maryland Battery

Artillery
McLaughlin's Battalion Maj. William McLaughlin
Chapman's (Virginia) Battery • Jackson's (Virginia) Battery

Hoke's Division Maj. Gen. Robert F. Hoke
Martin's Brigade Brig. Gen. James G. Martin
17th North Carolina • 42nd North Carolina • 66th North Carolina

Clingman's Brigade Brig. Gen. Thomas L. Clingman
8th North Carolina • 21st North Carolina • 51st North Carolina
61st North Carolina

Hagood's Brigade Brig. Gen. Johnson Hagood
11th South Carolina • 21st South Carolina • 25th South Carolina
27th South Carolina

Colquitt's Brigade Brig. Gen. Alfred H. Colquitt
6th Georgia • 19th Georgia • 23rd Georgia • 27th Georgia
28th Georgia

Artillery
Read's 38th Virginia Battalion Maj. John P. W. Read
Blount's (Virginia) Battery • Caskie's (Virginia) Battery
Macon's (Virginia) Battery • Marshall's (Virginia) Battery

CAVALRY CORPS Maj. Gen. Wade Hampton[11]
Hampton's Division Maj. Gen. Wade Hampton
Young's Brigade Col. Gilbert J. Wright
7th Georgia • Cobb's (Georgia) Legion • Phillips (Georgia) Legion
Jeff Davis (Mississippi) Legion • 20th Georgia Battalion

Rosser's Brigade Brig. Gen. Thomas L. Rosser
7th Virginia • 11th Virginia • 12th Virginia • 35th Virginia Battalion

---

9   Placed directly under Major General Breckenridge's command.
10   Placed under Brig. Gen. Lunsford L. Lomax's command.
11   No successor was officially named after Maj. Gen. J. E. B. Stuart's death on May 11.
Major General Wade Hampton, being the senior commissioned major general in the cavalry
corps, served in an acting role as head of the cavalry corps.

Butler's Brigade Brig. Gen. Matthew C. Butler
4th South Carolina • 5th South Carolina • 6th South Carolina
7th South Carolina[12]

Lee's Division Maj. Gen. Fitzhugh Lee
Lomax's Brigade Brig. Gen. Lunsford L. Lomax
5th Virginia • 6th Virginia • 15th Virginia

Wickham's Brigade Brig. Gen. Williams C. Wickham
1st Virginia • 2nd Virginia • 3rd Virginia • 4th Virginia

Lee's Division Maj. Gen. William H.F. Lee
Chambliss' Brigade Brig. Gen. John R. Chambliss
9th Virginia • 10th Virginia • 13th Virginia

Gordon's Brigade Col. John A. Baker,[13] Brig. Gen. Pierce M. B. Young
1st North Carolina • 2nd North Carolina • 3rd North Carolina
5th North Carolina

Horse Artillery Maj. R. Preston Chew
Breathed's Battalion Maj. James Breathed
Hart's (South Carolina) Battery • Johnston's (Virginia) Battery
McGregor's (Virginia) Battery • Shoemaker's (Virginia) Battery
Thomson's (Virginia) Battery

---

12   Technically operating under independent command after their arrival on May 29 to the army, but operated under Butler's command during the Cold Harbor actions.
13   Baker in command during some of the campaign; Brig. Gen. Pierce M. B. Young assumes command during latter stages.

Suggested Reading

THE BATTLE OF COLD HARBOR

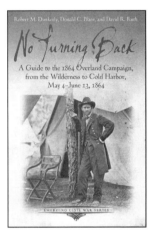

No Turning Back: A Guide to the 1864 Overland Campaign, from the Wilderness to Cold Harbor, May 4 – June 13, 1864
Robert M. Dunkerly, Donald C. Pfanz,
   and David R. Ruth
Savas Beatie, 2014 *(part of the Emerging Civil War Series)*
ISBN-13: 978-1611211931

A comprehensive overview of the entire campaign following the path set by the Virginia Civil War Trails system. Dunkerly, Pfanz, and Ruth—all National Park Service historians who have worked on the Overland Campaign's battlefields—offer a balanced, user-friendly guide to this critical campaign.

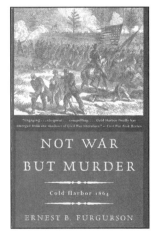

Not War But Murder: Cold Harbor 1864
Ernest B. Furgurson
Vintage, 2001
ISBN-13: 9780679455172

A highly readable account of the battle of Cold Harbor, *Not War But Murder* is not as minutely detailed as Gordon Rhea's book, but it's every bit as insightful.

A Season of Slaughter: The Battle of Spotsylvania Court House, May 8 – 21, 1864
Chris Mackowski and Kristopher D. White
Savas Beatie, 2013 *(part of the Emerging Civil War Series)*
ISBN-13: 978-1611211481

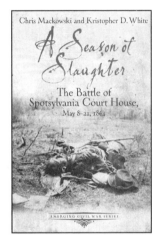

This prelude to *Hurricane from the Heavens* is a must-read for any interested enthusiast of the battle of Spotsylvania Court House. It's descriptive enough to paint the scene and informative enough to place you on the fields of battle. It includes a comprehensive driving tour so you can experience the sights that the soldiers struggled over for a fortnight in May 1863.

Cold Harbor, Grant and Lee, May 26 – June 5, 1864
Gordon C. Rhea
Louisiana State University Press, 2002
ISBN-13: 978-0807128039

The standard of battle narratives, Rhea's *Cold Harbor* is a complete study of the battles around Cold Harbor. It provides in-depth, tactical, and analytical insights into the entire campaign. Cold Harbor is the fourth (and last) volume in Rhea's mammoth study of the Overland Campaign.

About the Authors

Daniel T. Davis is a graduate of Longwood University, with a B.A. in Public History. Daniel has worked as a historian at both Appomattox Court House National Historic Site and at the Fredericksburg and Spotsylvania National Military Park. He has spoken at many Civil War Round Tables in the Mid-Atlantic Region. Daniel resides in Fredericksbug, VA, with his wife Katy and their Beagle mix, Bayla.

Phillip S. Greenwalt is currently employed as a historian for the National Park Service at George Washington Birthplace National Monument in Washington's Birthplace, Virginia and at Thomas Stone National Historic Site in Port Tobacco, Maryland. He worked as a historical intern at Fredericksburg and Spotsylvania National Military Park prior to his current position. He holds a bachelor degree in History from Wheeling Jesuit University and a graduate degree in American History from George Mason University. Phillip has taught at the community college level and has spoken regularly at Civil War and history round tables from the Mid-Atlantic to the Southeast to the Midwest. He currently lives on the historic Northern Neck of Virginia with his wife Adel and their rescue cat, Maya.

Daniel and Phill are the co-authors of the Emerging Civil War Series book *Bloody Autumn: The Shenandoah Valley Campaign of 1864*, and they are both regular contributors to the blog Emerging Civil War, www.emergingcivilwar.com.